Three Modern Novelists

Three Modern Novelists

Sōseki, Tanizaki, Kawabata

Van C. Gessel

Kodansha International
Tokyo • New York • London

A NOTE TO THE READER: Japanese names are given in Japanese order: given name preceded by surname.

Distributed in the United States by Kodansha America, Inc., 114 Fifth Avenue, New York, N.Y. 10011, and in the United Kingdom and continental Europe by Kodansha Europe Ltd., Gillingham House, 38–44 Gillingham Street, London SW1V 1HU. Published by Kodansha International Ltd., 17–14 Otowa 1–chome, Bunkyo-ku, Tokyo 112, and Kodansha America, Inc.

93 94 95 10 9 8 7 6 5 4 3 2 1

ISBN 4-7700-1652-2

Contents

Preface

Sōseki, Tanizaki, Kawabata. The names read like a roll call of the most important Japanese novelists of the twentieth century. With the exception of Mishima Yukio, whose flamboyant life has already been the subject of two full-length biographies and a motion picture in English, no other Japanese writers of the modern age are as well known in the West. Sōseki stands out as the first giant among novelists in Japan this century. And it was only death, it seems, that denied Tanizaki the Nobel Prize in literature that would go to Kawabata in 1968. Scholars, and even some armchair students of Japanese literature, have written a great deal about these three literary titans.

Why a biographical overview at this time of writers who are this familiar to a sophisticated international audience, and why in this format? I confess to having harbored some reservations myself when Michael Brase, my patient editor, first proposed the notion of this Kodansha Biography to me. I was quickly persuaded, however, once he described the intended audience.

This critical examination of the lives of these three extraordinary writers is aimed at the general, perhaps even the casual, reader of modern Japanese literature in English translation. Despite gloomy pronouncements by some scholars and publishers that there just "isn't a market" for Japanese literature (and, admittedly, the market comes to appear non-existent when figures on the Japanese readership of translated Western literature are cited in comparison), I remain convinced that new readers continue to discover and come under the sway of Japanese fiction. Those who keep track of such things have told me that my translation of Endō Shūsaku's 1980 novel *The Samurai*, sold something in the neighborhood of 13,000 copies in hardcover, and has gone through a half-dozen reprintings in paperback. And while it's certainly true that the three writers examined here are not the be-all and end-all of modern Japanese fiction, any reader who dips into the literature will ultimately have to take a look at the work of these masters.

The "general" audience I have envisioned consists, then, of individuals who have read a couple, even a handful, of Japanese novels in translation. Such readers, before venturing deeper, are bound to want to know something about the lives of the writers who have produced such extraordinary pieces of literature as *Kokoro*, *The Makioka Sisters*, and *The Sound of the Mountain*. Such background is almost vital for the understanding of the true breadth and brilliance of many Japanese works, far more so than with Western authors. I can quite happily proceed through an Updike novel without knowing the relationship between the author and his text. I admit, in fact, to knowing essentially nothing about Updike aside from the fact that he reviewed my first translation from Japanese in the *New Yorker*, which turned me into an instant Updike fan, though the review was not uncritical.

Such a luxury is not afforded the reader of Japanese literature. I realize this flies in the face of contemporary Western literary critical thinking, which insists that a text be surgically removed like a tumor from the author's being for discrete dissection. Works which cannot survive the operation are declared D.O.A. Any mention of the author's life brings cries that Oedipus's mother is being blamed for his sins. Nonetheless, I stand by my contention that Japanese fiction is written with the presumption that it will not be entirely severed from the life of the writer, and that readers will know something of the relationship between creator and creation. This is all part and parcel of the fundamentally autobiographical ("I"-centered) approach to literature that has been an integral part of the Japanese tradition since its inception.

This is not to suggest for a moment that any given novel cannot be read, appreciated, and understood without some knowledge of the novelist. Rather, I believe that a degree of information about the writer enhances an understanding of the fiction, makes the piece of writing more human, more "open," more susceptible to both emotional and critical response. That alone seems reason enough to present, in this compact, accessible form, the lives of Sōseki, Tanizaki, and Kawabata.

The fact that others have written much and well about these three writers means, of course, that some overlapping, some duplication of information is inevitable. I have tried to be scrupulous in detailing my sources of information, and to give credit to those remarkable scholars, the pioneers of Japanese literary studies in the West, whose writings I have drawn upon. I am grateful for what they have achieved, and indebted not only for specific details but for many forms of inspiration over the nearly two decades I have been involved with Japanese literature. I have, as well, quite naturally drawn upon the plentiful and enlightening Japanese sources, and these are also credited in the notes.

At the same time, every act of writing is an act of interpretation, and my approach to these three authors will, of necessity, be different from that of others. My perspectives, my responses, my interpretations must needs be individual, and it is my hope that I have done justice to the biographical subjects, to others who have written about them, and to my own critical thinking. Because of the stance I have tried to adopt toward each of these writers, I hope that each of the three chapters amounts to what the Japanese would call a *hyōden*, a "critical biography."

My approach can be seen as a study of each writer's response to the word that appears in each of the chapter titles: Modernity. Japan over the last hundred years has passed through stages of modernization that required centuries in other industrial nations. (In an attempt to illustrate both the tempo and the toll of Japan's modernization, one sardonic commentator, remarking on the current trade and racial friction between the US and Japan, recently quipped, "It took the British four hundred years to become arrogant; the Americans two hundred; the Japanese only two decades.") The pace of modernization inevitably created problems of dislocation, confusion, and resentment, and produced its share of social victims in an age of bewilderment.

To try to capture the sense of change, I have approached Natsume Sōseki as a writer who dealt in a profound way with the anguish that has attended Japan's move toward modernity. With Tanizaki, I have focused on his infatuation with the whole notion of the West, and the way he created an almost erotic ideal based on his sense of what the modern West was like. For Kawabata, it is his detachment from all around him, but in particular from a postwar Japan with which he felt increasingly uncomfortable, that seemed the most compelling approach to the man and his writings.

The experience of writing this book has been much more personally rewarding and informative than I ever imagined, and I am grateful to Michael Brase for spurring me to it. My single hope in making this manuscript available is that it enable the Western reader to appreciate more fully not only the men who produced the literature, but most importantly the remarkable novels themselves.

The Anguish of Modernity
Natsume Sōseki

At the end of 1984, the Japanese government began issuing a newly designed national currency, replacing all of the customary faces on its monetary bills. The public was naturally curious about the identities of the individuals who would take the place of such familiar visages as Prince Shōtoku (the first high-ranking official to patronize Buddhism in the seventh century) and a host of other political and mythological luminaries who had graced Japanese money for three decades. The face of Viscount Itō Hirobumi, one of the leading political manipulators of the Meiji period, was removed from the ¥1,000 bill. In his place, to be passed from hand to hand among the Japanese populace countless times each day, was printed the face of Japan's first world-class author in modern times, the novelist Natsume Sōseki.

It is not easy to imagine a Western parallel. Various individuals might be nominated for "best American writer," but it is hard to imagine much public enthusiasm for a $10 bill featuring Hawthorne or Melville (and how many Americans would recognize their likenesses?). And though Mark Twain might be a popular favorite, it wouldn't seem right to chuckle irreverently each time his face was hauled out to make a purchase. The problem becomes even thornier if we take into account the fact that Sōseki was a twentieth-century writer;

while the British might placidly welcome the appearance of Shakespeare or even Tennyson on their bills, one can hardly imagine them countenancing the selection of any modern novelist for such a distinction.

Japanese today have no such difficulties. Much more clearly than a Hawthorne or a Melville for America, Sōseki embodies many essential features of the most traumatic, most significant period of development in the history of modern Japan. For many Japanese, Sōseki is the experience of Japan in the Meiji period. Popular interest in his life and fiction continues at a level that we in the West usually sustain only for show business personalities. Etō Jun, one of the leading literary critics in Japan, recently commenced serialization of the third part of his monumental study, *Sōseki to sono jidai* (Sōseki and His Age), which he began writing in 1970. In 1990, a Yale-educated Japanese woman stirred up a discussion in Japan by publishing a 373-page "ending" to the novel *Meian* (Light and Darkness), which Sōseki left unfinished at his death in 1916. Recent public opinion surveys continue to rank several of Sōseki's major novels among works of literature which have had the most significant impact on the minds of Japanese students and intellectuals; in one such poll, *Kokoro* of 1914 ranked next to *Crime and Punishment*.

Sōseki remains for the Japanese today much more than the name of a writer anthologized in secondary school literature textbooks. Because he was born in 1867, the last year of the period usually labeled "pre-modern," his life and his writings, like Japan itself, directly confront the rapid Westernization that began at the end of the nineteenth century. Sōseki and his fictional characters do not approach Western ideas and innovations superficially; they probe into the intellectual core of meaning that this bi-cultural encounter entails. Nor do they brush off the anxieties of the age with smug self-assuredness; the distress they suffer as a result of the shifting dimensions of human relations comes through with stark clarity.

The attraction, then, of Sōseki's career and writings—even

for contemporary readers in Japan—is multifaceted. Born about a year before the major political upheavals which attended the Meiji Restoration in 1868, Sōseki's family heritage included training in the traditional Confucian standards of behavior. But if his initial upbringing was along conventional lines, his selection of English literature as a course of study, and his experiences living in England at the turn of the century, provided him with a catalog of alternative modes of living and thinking. Much of the human struggle that comes through in Sōseki's fiction is the battle between the old and the new, the Asian and the Western. These struggles are not waged in the abstract, however. Sōseki reduces them to the level of the individual, who is often confused or frightened.

The clash between the group-oriented behavior of Japanese tradition and the individual action of the West is one of the most evident of the conflicts, though by no means the only one, waged in Sōseki's stories. Sōseki perceived these clashes in terms of their impact on the individual life, but he is forever ambivalent as to appropriate solutions. He is unwilling to abandon completely the core and substance of traditional Japanese behavior, but is intelligent enough to see the benefits of individual freedom. Many of his fictional characters wander the uncharted lands lying between social responsibility and personal freedom, and many are ruined when they are unable to strike an easy balance between the two. After meandering through this no-man's land of torment, many Sōseki characters ultimately choose inaction, or sometimes even suicide. Such cultural ambivalence—or perhaps it would be better to call it moral ambivalence—lies at the heart of Sōseki's writing.

Natsume Sōseki, perhaps more distinctly than any other literary figure of his day, stood at the crossroads in the unfolding of modern Japan, and there he wavered. Convinced that it was crucial for the man of the new age to have a strong sense of individualism—though not necessarily one appropriated directly from the Western definition—Sōseki at the same time realized that the solitary path of individual liberty was often entered upon by acts of egotistical selfishness. His novels abound in betrayals, in the breaking of trusts, in the self-seeking rivalries that are the substance of love triangles.

And so, as the life of Natsume Sōseki unfolds, it will be useful to keep an eye open for small acts of betrayal as his parents shuffle him from one foster family to another; for lingering moments of loneliness as Sōseki retreats into his private world of study; for the perpetually gnawing doubts that plagued him in his quest to understand foreign literature; for his attempts to understand how Japan could modernize without merely aping the West. The ambivalence and torment of his fictional characters are often and in many ways reflections of the agonies besetting Sōseki the man as well.

* * *

Natsume Kinnosuke (Sōseki was a pen name adopted later) was born February 9, 1867, in the Ushigome district of the city of Edo, a little over a year before it was renamed Tokyo and established as the national capital under the Restoration regime. He was the fifth son and eighth child born into the family, though an older brother and sister had previously died in infancy. This was not an inordinately large family for the time, but circumstances combined to make the birth of this child an unwelcome event. The family heads were not members of the privileged samurai class, but they claimed the hereditary position of *nanushi*, a kind of village headman. Though they could not have known it at the time, the position of *nanushi* would soon be abolished by the new Meiji government, but for the short term the addition of a new child did not pose any immediate economic problems. It seems far more likely that the new infant was not welcomed because his parents considered the family already complete. Kinnosuke was a late addition, born when his father was over fifty and his mother forty. Apparently this was a social embarrassment to the family, and the readiest solution was to farm the boy out to another family. In naming the child, his father, believing perhaps in the age-old astrological custom of selecting auspicious names, dubbed him Kinnosuke, the *kin* character (which means gold) being considered a talisman to ward off troubles.

The family who initially took charge of the infant operated a used-goods shop (some accounts say it was a greengrocer's) in the Yotsuya district of Edo. Running the business seemed to occupy much of their energies, and Kinnosuke was placed in a basket and set out in front of the shop to keep him out of the way. His cries of hunger and discomfort were ignored until an older half-sister of Kinnosuke's from the Natsume family, passing the shop one night, took pity on him. She picked up the child and took him back to his real home, doubt less reporting the heartless treatment he had been receiving. The parents permitted the child to remain in the house, but stood firm in their determination to eventually place the child elsewhere. Within a year or so, Kinnosuke was formally adopted by Shiobara Masanosuke, who had boarded with the Natsume family in his school days. Shiobara and his wife, Yasu, who had formerly been a servant in the Natsume household, had no children of their own.

Kinnosuke's new foster parents were good to him, showering him with gifts and doting on him as he passed through his formative years. But apparently this love for the child compensated for the lack of love they felt toward each other. In his own recollections, Sōseki wrote that his childhood years had "a cold and sad shadow over them,"[1] and the hostility between the Shiobaras only mounted as the child grew older. In 1874 Yasu discovered that her husband was having an affair, and she took Kinnosuke and returned for a brief time to the Natsume house. Soon, however, she was reconciled with Masanosuke, and the boy was started in school. Two years later, the situation once again grew intolerable, and the couple were divorced. Kinnosuke, who was nine, was once more returned to the Natsume family. By now, the impact of disenfranchisement as village headman and the decline of family fortunes had taken its toll, and the reappearance of an extra child could not have been welcomed. The fact that the three older brothers in the Natsume family, who by this time were in their late teens or early twenties, were living profligate lives and displayed little interest in bolstering the family's situation did not help matters. Two of these brothers, in fact, would die almost simultaneously of pneumonia in another ten years. As far as the nine-year-old Kinnosuke was concerned, he had no clear idea at first how he was related to this strange new family, a fact that could only have served to heighten his sense of displacement.

In a memoir written not long before his death, Sōseki recalled his traumatic childhood:

> I was born to my parents in their evening years. I was their youngest son. The story that my mother was ashamed of having a baby at her age I hear even now.... At any rate, I was sent soon afterward to a certain couple as their adopted son.... I was with them until the age of eight or nine, when one begins to understand things. There was some trouble between them, so it was arranged that I should be returned to my parents.... I did not know that I had come back to my own home, and I went on thinking as I did before that my parents were my grandparents. Unsuspectingly I continued to call them "grandma" and "grandpa." They, on their part, thinking perhaps that it would be strange to change things suddenly, said nothing when I called them this. They did not pet me as parents do their youngest children.... I remember that my father treated me rather harshly.... One night, the following incident took place. I was sleeping alone in a room when I was awakened by someone calling my name in a quiet voice. Frightened, I looked at the figure crouching by my bedside. It was dark, so I could not tell who it was. Being a child, I lay still and listened to what the person had to say. Then I realized that the voice belonged to our maid. In the darkness, the maid whispered into my ear: "These people that

you think are your grandfather and grandmother are really your father and mother. I am telling you this because recently I heard them saying that you must in some way have sensed that they were your parents since you seemed to prefer this house to the other one. They were saying how strange it was. You mustn't tell anybody that I told you this. Understand?" All I said at the time was "All right," but in my heart I was happy. I was happy not because I had been told the truth, but because the maid had been so kind to me.[2]

Kinnosuke had not seen the last of his foster father, however. When in 1877 Shiobara married his lover, who had a daughter from a previous marriage, he conceived the idea of having Kinnosuke eventually marry this young woman and take over the household, since legally he was still registered as the adopted son of the Shiobaras. Nothing came of that hope. But more than twenty-five years later, if Sōseki's autobiographical account in the novel *Michikusa* (Grass on the Wayside, 1915; trans. 1969) is to be given any credibility, Shiobara still retained hopes of luring Kinnosuke back into his family, and after a chance encounter following Sōseki's return from London, he began importuning his foster son, now a respected scholar, for money.

Though all accounts suggest that Kinnosuke's natural father continued to regard the boy as a financial nuisance after his return to the household, his mother, Chie, appears to have welcomed him back and treated him with warmth. A fervent theatergoer, she had often taken her daughters to the Kabuki, and after Kinnosuke's arrival he accompanied her to listen to *rakugo* performers—comic storytellers who were noted for their crisp, infectious colloquial style. The writer Sōseki would learn much from these raconteurs, and the typically Edo brashness of their delivery and the rhythms of their colloquial language are evident in his writing, especially in such early humorous works as *Wagahai wa neko de aru* (I Am a Cat, 1905–6; trans. 1961) and *Botchan* (Botchan, 1906; trans. 1972). Kinnosuke was fourteen when his mother died.

By the time Kinnosuke moved on to middle school, which was two years after his mother's death, the curriculum in Japanese schools had changed considerably. Over a decade had elapsed since the Meiji Restoration, and the doors of Japan had been opened wide to all manner of innovations from the West. Kinnosuke found two separate scholastic tracks being offered. One was the "main" curriculum, emphasizing traditional modes of study. The other, considered the more progressive track, was designed for those who wished to ride the crest of interest in things Western and focused on English-language study. Although he cannot have been unaffected by the widespread enthusiasm for Western studies—the possibility of wealth and riches in the new era must have been an avid topic among his classmates—Kinnosuke remained adamantly opposed to this approach to education. He despised the English language, and rejected the view that the study of the West would automatically translate into financial success. He consequently opted for the main curriculum.

It was at middle school that Kinnosuke encountered Chinese literature, and it was then that his early love for the literary arts was fostered. He became absorbed in the reading of Chinese poetry and fiction, and memorized thousands of lines of Chinese poetry from the Tang and Song periods. His familiarity with Chinese classical literature sparked his first thoughts of becoming a writer. But when he told one of his dissolute elder brothers, he was scoffed at. In an age when virtually every young man who pursued a career did so to rise in the world and to contribute something to the national effort of "enlightenment," literature—particularly Asian literature—was considered one of the least likely paths to success. Kinnosuke's brother informed him in no uncertain terms that writing was a skill that he might cultivate, but in no way was it a profession. A "profession" meaning, of course, an occupation that would benefit the nation as well as oneself; a "skill," something that could only enhance the individual. Such selfish attainments were frivolous at best, unpatriotic at worst.

Kinnosuke appears to have been persuaded by his brother's logic, because by the time he completed middle school in 1883, he had concluded that he needed to continue his education and pursue something of more practical value. His earlier aversion to the study of English giving way to a desire to make something of himself in the new society, he enrolled in a preparatory school to improve his knowledge of English. It would appear that he received minimal financial assistance from his family to do so. In 1884 he left home to move into an apartment with a friend, where he began his studies for the university entrance examinations.

In September of that year, Kinnosuke was accepted at the college of Tokyo University. His career goal at this point in time—certainly more practical than the study of classical literature—was to become an architect. But again he seems to have been flexible and willing to listen to others. When he confided to a school friend that he had chosen architecture because, while he recognized that he was a peculiar fellow, he felt he could continue in his peculiar ways as an architect while making money at the same time, his classmate employed an argument that would later echo faintly in Sōseki's novel *Sorekara* (And Then, 1909; trans. 1978). Japan, the friend said, was such an impoverished nation that it could never hope to compete with the great and wealthy countries of the West. Everything Japan might attempt would pale in comparison. A Japanese architect, for instance, could never hope to build anything that would begin to rival a timeless edifice like St. Paul's. Such competition was simply out of poor Japan's league. As Sōseki wrote in *And Then*, "Japan can't get along without borrowing from the West. But it poses as a first-class power. And it's straining to join the ranks of the first-class powers. That's why, in every direction, it puts up the facade of a first-class power and cheats on what's behind."[3] A writer, on the other hand, would not be subjected to the standards of wealth or poverty, and even in a land as wanting as Japan one could attain the stature of a great writer.[4] Once again literature presented itself to Sōseki as the kind of career he might find congenial, the kind of occupation in which he might hope to succeed despite Japan's lowly station.

It was at this point in his life that ill health began to plague Kinnosuke. Shortly after he enrolled in the college, he developed appendicitis. By 1886 he was having ulcer attacks, perhaps prompted by his failure in an examination to move up in his class. The urge to succeed, a self-impelled drive to make something of his life, appears to have taken its toll on Sōseki's health throughout his career. Failure at this point served its purpose, forcing him to make a solemn vow to succeed at his studies. It was a vow he kept, remaining thereafter at the top of his class until graduation. He also came to the decision that he would no longer be a financial drain on his family. He picked up a job as a part-time teacher (lecturing in English on geometry at a private academy) to see himself through school.

In 1887, the year that two of his elder brothers succumbed to pneumonia, Kinnosuke had an attack of acute trachoma. The condition became so severe that his parents had him taken from his dormitory and brought home, confounding his resolve to be independent. Trachoma remained a chronic problem and required frequent visits to an ophthalmologist.

In 1888, living at home once again and studying hard so that he could eventually stand on his own feet, Kinnosuke had his name legally changed from Shiobara to Natsume. Hoping to put an end once and for all to his relationship with his foster father, he wrote a letter informing him of the action and sent ¥240 as a sort of severance payment. Commentators suggest that the move was occasioned by the deaths of his two brothers and the failure of the remaining elder brother to prove himself capable of putting aside his profligate ways and assuming the position of legal heir: in short, that Kinnosuke's action was intended to prepare himself for that role. It is ironic that the son whom the family had been at such pains to dispose of should be the one who turned out most fit to inherit the family name.

That same year, Kinnosuke completed his studies at the college and was admitted into the literature department at the First Upper Middle School (later to be known as Tokyo Imperial University), where he met a man who would encourage his literary aspirations, Masaoka Shiki. The two men remained friends for life, though Shiki, who became Japan's first great modern haiku poet, would die young of consumption. Shiki provided encouragement to Sōseki as he began his pursuit of literature, amending Sōseki's haiku and founding the literary magazine *Hototogisu*, which would publish Sōseki's first fiction.

By 1889 Shiki had already begun coughing up blood, and it was in a get-well letter to Shiki that Kinnosuke composed his first haiku poem. While the two of them were sending poetry manuscripts back and forth, Kinnosuke first used the pen name "Sōseki." The name, like many sobriquets chosen by writers in the Meiji period, seems to have been selected somewhat facetiously: taken from a classical Chinese text, it can mean someone who is either "eccentric" or "obstinate." Since he had earlier described his interest in architecture as the result of his "peculiar" nature, it is perhaps no surprise that he continued to regard himself as a recalcitrant eccentric as he continued his studies of literature. Along with haiku, Sōseki also began to produce *kanshi*, poetry written in classical Chinese. Though some modern critics have little respect for Sōseki's haiku, he is still regarded by many as the greatest master of *kanshi* that Japan has produced in this century.

In 1890 Sōseki entered the English literature department at Tokyo Imperial University. One of his classmates, Yamada Bimyō, and three upperclassmen—Kawakami Bizan, Ozaki Kōyō, and Ishibashi Shian—later formed a literary group known as the Friends of the Inkstone (Ken'yūsha) and published Japan's first modern literary journal while still at college. The English literature department at Tokyo Imperial University was a new program, having been founded only a year earlier and producing only one graduate before Kinno-

suke came along. As the program's second student, Kinnosuke read a good deal of Western literature, hoping someday,
he wrote, "to startle the Westerners by producing terrific
works written in foreign languages."[5] Though he merely toyed
with the idea of startling Westerners with an introduction to
the culture of Japan, it is clear that Sōseki had strengthened
his determination to become a writer. It is equally clear that he
was less than pleased with the literary training he received at
the university. In a letter to Shiki he complained that after undertaking the academic study of literature, his initial passion
for the subject of English literature had completely collapsed.
Much of the blame, it would appear, must fall on the shoulders of the British lecturer who had been hired to teach the
subject at the university. As Sōseki himself told an audience
of university students in 1914:

> At the university, I majored in English literature. What
> exactly is English literature, you may well ask. I myself did
> not know the answer to that after three years of furious study.
> Our instructor in those days was Professor Dixon. He would
> make us read poetry aloud, read prose passages to him, do
> composition; he would scold us for dropping articles, angrily
> explode when we mispronounced things. His exam questions
> were always of one kind: give Wordsworth's birth and death
> dates, give the number of Shakespeare's folios, list the works
> of Scott in chronological order.... Can this be English litera-
> ture? Is this any way to instill an understanding of what litera-
> ture is, English or otherwise? All right, you say, forge
> through on your own. But this is like the proverbial blind man
> peeking through the fence. I would wander about in the li-
> brary searching for something that would give me a start. But
> there was nothing. This was not simply because I lacked mo-
> tivation; the field was represented by the most meager collec-
> tion of books. For three years I studied, and at the end I still
> did not know what literature was. This, I might say, was the
> source of my agony.[6]

However badly he was taught concerning the true nature
of literature, Sōseki had, in fact, mastered the English lan-

guage and developed a genuine awareness of its literary potentiality. In 1891 Professor Dixon asked him to produce a translation of one of the major texts in classical Japanese literature, the thirteenth-century *Hōjōki* (Record of My Ten-Foot-Square Hut) by Kamo no Chōmei. Sōseki's sensitivity to the potentialities and nuances of literature are evident in his prefatory essay, where he writes (in English):

> The literary products of a genius contain everything. They are a mirror in which every one finds his image, reflected with startling exactitude; they are a fountain which quenches the thirst of fiery passion, refreshes a dull, dejected spirit, cools the hot care-worn temples and infuses into all a subtle sense of pleasure all but spiritual; an elixir inspiring all, a tonic elevating all minds.[7]

His translation of *Hōjōki* is remarkable for its time, and impressive for any time. While his style is heavily influenced by the mode of writing acquired from his study of English literature, his facility and versatility remain nothing short of astonishing. He renders the famous opening passage of the work, which students of Japanese literature throughout the world still dutifully commit to memory, as follows:

> Incessant is the change of water where the stream glides on calmly: the spray appears over a cataract, yet vanishes without a moment's delay. Such is the fate of men in the world and of the houses in which they live. Walls standing side by side, tilings vying with one another in loftiness, these are from generations past the abodes of high and low in a mighty town. But none of them has resisted the destructive work of time. Some stand in ruins; others are replaced by new structures. Their possessors too share the same fate with them.[8]

Such passages offer concrete evidence that Sōseki was being overly modest when he claimed he had no ear for English poetry.[9] And though some critics have denigrated Sōseki's dozen or so original forays, some of it can be quite affecting, such as the following, written in August 1903, seven months after Sōseki's return from England:

Dawn of Creation

Heaven in her first grief said: "Wilt thou kiss me once
    more ere we part?"
"Yes dear," replied Earth. "A thousand kisses,
    if they cure thee of thy grief."
They slept a while, souls united in each other's
    embrace.
They were one; no Heaven and no Earth yet,
When lo! there came Thunder to lash them
    out of slumber.
It was in the dawn of creation, and they have
    never met since.
Now they live wide apart:
And though the pale moon never tires to send her silent
    message with her melancholy light,
Though all the stars wink and beckon night after night,
Though all the tears fall mute and fresh to crystallise
    her sorrow on every blade,
They have never met since.
Alas! Earth is beset with too many sins to meet her.[10]

For all his talents, Sōseki remained a pessimist, and on top of his frustrations with the pedagogical approach at school, he was also to experience around this time his first encounter with disappointed love. In 1891 he was attracted to a woman he had met at the ophthalmologist's, but a relationship failed to develop. And perhaps more significantly, his sister-in-law, Tose, died from a particularly severe case of morning sickness later that same year. One prominent Sōseki critic in Japan has boldly speculated that Tose was Sōseki's "secret love," and that the profound, misanthropic depression he sank into after her death was brought on by a combined sense of loss and guilt. Whether this imaginative supposition is justified will

likely never be resolved. Critics for decades have been search-
ing for some pattern in Sōseki's personal life which would account for all the love triangles and betrayals that abound in his
fiction, and a relationship with his sister-in-law would certainly fill that prescription. For our purposes here, it is sufficient
to note that frustration with what was happening in the classroom, insecurity about his own abilities in English, a growing
pessimism about the possibility of understanding the essence
of literature, and the loss of two women he may have cared
very deeply about, combined to send Sōseki into a spiraling
depression, a bout of mental anguish that would recur at many
points throughout his later life.

Despite (or perhaps because of) this depression, Sōseki
was particularly active during his penultimate year as an un-
dergraduate in 1892. He took on a part-time teaching position
to defray the costs of schooling. He produced an essay on one
school of Chinese philosophy, and joined the editorial staff of
a journal of philosophical studies. During his summer vacation, he and Masaoka Shiki, who had dropped out of school
after failing his exams, traveled to Kyoto and other cities in
western Japan. They subsequently visited Matsuyama, where
Shiki had several poet friends, including Takahama Kyoshi,
who would play a part in publishing some of Sōseki's first
writings.

As part of his continuing exploration of the meaning of literature, Sōseki wrote an essay titled, "On the Poems of Walt
Whitman, a Representative Egalitarian Writer," which appeared in the journal he helped to edit. This essay was probably the first introduction of Whitman and his poetry to Japan,
although the article went largely unnoticed, appearing as it did
in a journal with limited circulation. Sōseki followed up this
work the next year with an essay titled, "Nature as Viewed by
the English Poets." This perceptive study, presented first as a
lecture at the university and subsequently committed to print,
is no mere catalog of British poetic responses to objects of nature, but an insightful and persuasive examination of the de-

velopment of literary attitudes. In his concluding summary, Sōseki writes:

> Poets in the age of Pope did not experience nature direct-ly. They nurtured their poetic conceptions by toying with an-cient vocabulary. Goldsmith and Cowper loved nature for it-self. The Naturalism of Thomson was mere objectivity, and often included elements of drabness. Burns through the emo-tions and Wordsworth through the intellect, both compare na-ture to active energy.[11]

The examples of poetry cited suggest a wide familiarity with English verse and a critical edge to Sōseki's thinking. His presentation of this lecture, followed by its publication as an essay, attracted more attention than his earlier work on Whitman and eventually led to requests for critical manu-scripts by other magazines.

In 1893, the year his article on British poets appeared, Sōseki graduated from the English literature department. Though he was only the second student to complete the de-gree, he continued to feel inadequate in his knowledge of his major subject, and managed to persuade himself that it was impossible for a foreigner ever to master British literature. In fact, he struggled, as he put it, with "a feeling of insecurity, as if he had been deceived by English literature."[12] Perhaps it was a combination of such feelings of intellectual deficiency and the lack of compelling alternatives that impelled Sōseki to en-roll in the graduate program of his department. He simultane-ously took on a second teaching job, signing up as a lecturer in the English language at the Tokyo Normal School. His re-action to that appointment is strikingly similar to the ambiva-lent attitude his fictional hero Botchan would later take toward the teaching profession: Sōseki remarked, "It was suggested to me that I should teach. I had no desire to teach, or not to teach."[13] Similarly, Sōseki and Botchan both felt incapable of providing a model of moral conduct for their students. Sōseki describes his encounter with Kanō Jigorō, head of the

Normal School, after he had been made an offer.

> I even attempted to convince President Kanō of my un-
> worthiness. I insisted that I was unfit to teach at the Normal
> School if what he had said was true—that as a teacher I must
> be a model for the students. But he went me one better: hear-
> ing me decline with such simple honesty, he said, made him
> want me all the more. He refused to let me go. And so I
> ended up taking the job at the Normal School.... So now I
> had the job, but the fact was that I had never been qualified to
> make anything of myself as an educator, and at school I felt
> nervous and inferior. Perhaps I could have shirked my duties
> if I had been cleverer; Mr. Kanō complained that I was too
> simple and honest. But I could not escape the feeling that I
> was in the wrong place. Quite frankly, I felt like a fishmonger
> working in a pastry shop.... With this ambivalent attitude, I
> emerged from school to take my place in the world. I be-
> came—or rather, was made into—a teacher. Questionable as
> my language ability was, I knew enough to get along and
> managed to squeak by each day. Deep inside, however, I
> knew only emptiness. No, perhaps if it had been emptiness I
> could have resigned myself more completely, but there was
> something continually bothering me, some vague, disagree-
> able, half-formed thing that would not let me alone. To make
> matters worse, I felt not the slightest interest in my work as a
> teacher. I had known from the start that I was no educator,
> but I saw it was hopeless when just teaching English classes
> seemed like an enormous burden. I was always in a crouch,
> ready to spring into my true calling as soon as the slightest
> opening should present itself. But this "true calling" of mine
> was something that seemed to be there and at the same time
> was not. No matter where I turned, I could not bring myself
> to make the plunge.[14]

Early in 1894 Sōseki coughed up blood after a serious cold
that showed signs of degenerating into pneumonia. Whether
this was due to the strain of working at two jobs while he pursued an advanced degree, depression over what he perceived
as his own shortcomings as both student and teacher, a painful
triangular love affair which some critics have posited between

Sōseki and a classmate, or a combination of these pressures, we cannot know. In any event, afraid that he might come down with tuberculosis, Sōseki curtailed his writing activities and devoted his energies to recuperation. He spent time at the scenic northern area of Matsushima, sought solace in the poetry of Shelley, and took up the study of archery, perhaps to focus his attention and calm his nerves. At the end of the year, he secluded himself at the Enkakuji Buddhist temple in Kamakura for a period of two months, where he studied Zen meditation. By his own account, and as can be inferred from his novel *Mon* (The Gate, 1910; trans. as *Mon* in 1972), Sōseki derived neither comfort nor enlightenment from his attempts to pass through the gate of religious wisdom toward greater understanding of himself and his life. Evidently the sole worldly benefit he sought to gain from his experience with Buddhist mediation was a position as a reporter for the English-language newspaper *Japan Mail*, which was published in Yokohama. Early in 1895 Sōseki wrote an article in English on the practice of Zen which he sent as part of his application to the paper. The editors there were not sufficiently edified by its contents to add Sōseki to their staff.

In April of 1895, "in the spirit of renouncing everything"[15] (perhaps after all there had been a moment of illumination that came to him at Enkakuji!), Sōseki resigned both of his teaching positions and accepted a position as English teacher at the Ehime Prefecture Middle School on the rural island of Shikoku. This would not be the only time in his career that Sōseki held his nose and leaped blindly from a precipice; he took a similarly courageous jump in 1907.

The offer from the middle school in the city of Matsuyama was not an unattractive one: with a wage of ¥80 per month, Sōseki the newcomer would not only be the best-paid teacher at the school, he would also be receiving a higher salary than the principal. But some part of his decision to jettison respectable academic appointments in the capital (prestigious because of their central location) to go to the "sticks" must be attributed to Sōseki's upstart, "eccentric" nature. He could not have known that several months after his arrival in Matsuyama, his old school friend and literary confidante, Masaoka Shiki, would return ill from a stint as war reporter with the Japanese troops fighting the Sino-Japanese War and settle for a time in Matsuyama. Nor would he have had the prescience to know that he would be engaged to be married during his brief stay in Matsuyama. So, as incomprehensible as his personal exile might have seemed to his comrades in Tokyo, Sōseki's half-desperate flight to the hinterlands ended up providing him with both stimulation for his literary career and a wife.

Although the portrait painted of Matsuyama middle school students in the droll novel *Botchan* is less than favorable, Sōseki apparently got along well with both his students and the school administrators, and there are no grounds for attempting to read the novel as wholly accurate in such details. It is equally clear, however, that Sōseki did not like living so far from the center of culture. But thanks to his old friend Shiki, he was able to create a bit of culture of his own in his new home. Shiki lived with Sōseki for two months after his return from the battlefield and encouraged his teacher friend to continue writing poetry. Sōseki consequently began publishing both haiku and Chinese verses in a variety of newspapers and magazines, joined an association of haiku poets at his school called the Wind in the Pines Society, and fostered an acquaintance with another poet friend of Shiki's, Takahama Kyoshi. Over two-thirds of the 2,400 haiku Sōseki composed in his lifetime were produced during the four years beginning with his stay in Matsuyama.[16]

During his winter vacation from school, Sōseki traveled up to Tokyo and there had an arranged marriage interview (*miai*) with Nakane Kyōko, the daughter of the chief clerk for the House of Peers in the Japanese parliament. Sōseki, who had already rejected earlier proposals, was attracted to Kyōko because "though she had bad teeth, she made no attempt to hide them."[17] For her part, Kyōko was pleased with the impression left by Sōseki in comparison to previous prospects: "... none of the photographs had impressed me so favorably as to induce me to commit myself to marriage. Besides, it would seem that my father was not too enthusiastic about any of the suitors. But this particular party, when I saw the photograph, pleased me very much. There was a gentlemanly and quietly settled air about him. His eyes were steady, and there was on his face a calm and trustworthy expression."[18] Negotiations to confirm the betrothal went smoothly, and Sōseki seemed in better spirits when he returned to Matsuyama in January of 1896.

A circle of disciples began to form around Sōseki while he was in Matsuyama, some of whom remained attached to him for life. Initially, of course, these were local haiku writers who admired Sōseki's abilities as a poet. In later years Sōseki would continue to be surrounded by a respectful and fiercely loyal following. He was a generous literary mentor, regularly devoting time from his schedule to meet and discuss literature with his followers, fostering the works of talented newcomers, and providing even those with opposing views of literature space in the literary newspaper column he wrote. The successful careers of several of the most prominent writers of the 1920s, including Akutagawa Ryūnosuke, owe much to the early mentoring offered by Sōseki.

In April 1896 Sōseki resigned his position at the Matsuyama middle school after only a year of teaching. His departure appears not to have been motivated by the same sense of moral outrage that drives Botchan from Matsuyama, for there are no reports of conflicts with his peers. Nor was it mere nostalgia for the capital that prompted the move: for in the fall Sōseki took up a teaching position at the Fifth High School in Kumamoto, a Kyushu city even further removed from the center of cultural activity in Tokyo. A new monthly salary of ¥100, a ¥20 increase over his Matsuyama pay, seems hardly adequate to explain the move. The perpetual restlessness—or perhaps it should be termed uneasiness—that tormented Sōseki throughout his life may have played a role. In any case, the monthly ¥100 was not all his to spend. Ten of it was sent regularly to his natural father, another three to his older sister Fusa (actually a half-sister borne to his father's first wife, the sister who retrieved the infant Kinnosuke from outside the neglectful greengrocer's shop).

After spending some time with his friends and disciples in Matsuyama, Sōseki set out for Kumamoto in mid-April. In June, his fiancée's father escorted her to Kumamoto, and Sōseki and Kyōko were married there on the tenth of June. It was, in many respects, a bad union for both of them. Kyōko in her memoirs recalls that Sōseki's first words to her after the ceremony were: "I am a scholar and therefore must study. I have no time to fuss over you. Please understand this."[19] His apparent unwillingness to bend from his stern attitude was matched by her regular bouts of hysteria, which intensified when she was ill or pregnant—and she bore seven children in addition to having at least one miscarriage. The profound fits of depression were paralleled by Sōseki's mental imbalance, which occasionally veered toward full-blown derangement. Their instabilities must have chafed and fed upon one another, leading to a permanent rift.

When Sōseki the novelist wrote about wedded couples in his later fiction, the portraits were invariably shaded by his own unhappy marriage relationship. One need only think of the walls that Sensei builds between himself and his wife in *Kokoro*, barriers that ultimately force him to choose suicide over sharing his innermost fears and feelings with her. Michiyo's loveless marriage to Hiraoka in *Sorekara*; Kenzō's inability in *Michikusa* to express affection for his wife in any form other than irritation; the gentle love between Sōsuke and Oyone in *Mon*, painted with hues of quiet despair—surely such depictions of man and wife bear some of the burden of the unhappiness in Sōseki's own married life.

Perhaps the barrier of austerity that Sōseki built between

himself and Kyōko the moment after they had spoken their vows was in part an expression of his frustration with other aspects of his life. He continued to be unhappy as an English teacher, sensing somehow that he was perpetrating a fraud, and though he had achieved modest success as a haiku poet in Matsuyama, his dreams of becoming a serious writer seemed doomed to failure as he took on the responsibilities of a family in a remote part of Japan. A portion of that disappointment he channeled into the writing of Chinese *kanshi*, which at this point became his primary mode of literary expression. It would again assume a dominant position in his life in the painful months preceding his death.

The four years Sōseki spent in Kumamoto were tinged with anguish. In June of 1897 his natural father died. This was followed by the selling of the family house, toward which Sōseki must have felt a mixture of emotions, but which incidentally allowed him to pay off his school debts and achieve a degree of financial comfort he had not previously experienced. Earlier in the year he had turned down an offer arranged by his influential father-in-law to teach at a school in Tokyo. Not that he did not want to return to the capital—in fact, the offer only whetted his desire to do so—but because he yearned for some opening that would enable him to break free from the prison-house of teaching.

In early July of 1897 Sōseki took his pregnant wife to spend their summer vacation in Tokyo. Her family was there, and could tend to her needs. Undoubtedly he hoped to continue establishing contacts in the Tokyo literary world and sniff out any career options that might allow him to pursue his writing. Soon after their arrival, however, Kyōko had a miscarriage. As severe as the physical repercussions may have been, the emotional toll on Kyōko was enormous, high-strung as she already was. The two went to spend the remainder of the summer in Kamakura, where she would have a chance to recuperate, and the bulk of Sōseki's vacation was spent commuting between Tokyo and Kamakura, together with visits to Masaoka Shiki in his sickbed and calls on the priest at Enkakuji who had earlier guided him in Zen meditation. When the new school year began in September, Sōseki returned alone to Kumamoto, where Kyōko joined him the following month. During his break at the end of the year, Sōseki spent time at a hot springs that would be the setting for his 1906 novel *Kusamakura* (Pillow of Grass; trans. as *The Three-Cornered World*, 1965).

One of the few positive moments during that traumatic year came when the editors of a literary journal published in Tokyo requested a critical article. They had read his 1893 essay "Nature as Viewed by the English Poets," and been impressed by it, but could not understand why so talented a critic had disappeared from the literary landscape. When they discovered that Sōseki was teaching in Kumamoto, they contacted him and persuaded him to write a study of Laurence Sterne's *Tristram Shandy*, which they published in March. A second literary event, tangential to Sōseki's career at this point but later important, was the January 1897 establishment of the literary journal *Hototogisu* by some of Sōseki's Matsuyama literary cronies from the "Wind in the Pines Society." Masaoka Shiki was the key figure at the journal, but Takahama Kyoshi took the lead in badgering Sōseki to contribute; the following year, after the site of publication shifted from Matsuyama to Tokyo, Sōseki complied by producing an essay. His association with the magazine remained intimate for many years: they published not only his critical writings on British literature but also some of his poetry, portions of his account of his sojourn in England, and three of his first four novels. (It is intriguing that the one early novel, *Kusamakura*, which Sōseki himself labeled a "haiku-like" work, is the one not serialized in *Hototogisu*, though the journal was founded by haiku poets and largely devoted to such composition.)

One of the main reasons that Shiki and Kyoshi were persistent in requesting an article from Sōseki was their realization that he was growing increasingly despondent in Kumamoto. Increasingly he had the sense that his career track was like a merry-go-round, revolving in concentric circles and leading nowhere. Though he had been promoted at the high school, many men his age were already school principals. Around the same period, a rival scholar published an "introductory" essay on the poetry of Walt Whitman in the Waseda University papers series without acknowledging Sōseki's much earlier study. This of course only heightened Sōseki's sense that he was removed from the literary circles he yearned to be part of. Simultaneously, many of his closest friends in Kumamoto were beginning to move away to pursue other activities.[20]

Sōseki's feelings of isolation were in no way assuaged by the atmosphere at home. Kyōko's mental condition since her miscarriage had deteriorated markedly. She had been subject to hysterical fits for many months, and in June of 1898, almost a year after the tragedy, she attempted suicide by throwing herself into the Shirakawa river near their home in Kumamoto. Some fishermen who were net-fishing in the swollen river managed to rescue her, and an acquaintance at the school kept the incident out of the papers.

In his late autobiographical novel, *Michikusa*, Sōseki describes how the protagonist Kenzō would tie the *obi* of his nightdress to his wife's each night before they went to sleep, afraid that she might slip away and try again to do harm to herself. Some biographers believe that Sōseki actually did this with Kyōko. Once again, he turned to the writing of *kanshi* to palliate his feelings of futility.

After they had moved to a house away from the river, Kyōko began to show signs of recovery, but the double-edged sword of a second pregnancy cut its way into their relationship. The hope of bringing a child safely into the world to replace the lost one was offset by attacks of severe morning sickness. That illness triggered in Kyōko a hysterical dread that she might lose yet another baby, and her mental attacks resumed with a fury. Sōseki spent his days and nights in terror.

By November of that year, however, the nausea subsided, and with it Kyōko's anxiety. A semblance of normalcy was restored in the Natsume home, and in May of 1899 the first child, a daughter, was safely delivered. Sōseki had turned thirty-two earlier that year, and his lingering aspiration to become a writer was memorialized in the name he gave his daughter: Fudeko, "child of the writing brush." Around the time Fudeko was born, Sōseki began to study the chanted singing style of Nō drama known as *utai*; the chronology here is unclear, so it is impossible to tell whether he did this in quest of solace during Kyōko's hysteria or in relief at the normal birth. Such a hobby was by no means unusual for a man of culture in Sōseki's day, but those who heard him perform declared him unusually inept. The female novelist Nogami Yaeko, his literary disciple, claimed he sounded distinctly like a mountain goat.[21]

Kyōko's memoirs record a lighter moment from Sōseki's experience of this period. He owned a large dog that barked incessantly, irritating the neighbors. But one day the animal bit a passerby, and the police were summoned. Rather than docilely surrendering his dog to the authorities for rabies tests, Sōseki took on the officer instead. He insisted that dogs were perceptive creatures, barking because they detect something suspicious, and biting only inferior types or people with a particular disliking for dogs. The policeman, nonplused by this reasoning, could only reply that a human being is more valuable than a dog, and took the animal off to be tested. The dog was returned to the Natsumes early the next morning with a clean bill of health and a warning that he would be destroyed if he ever attacked again.

Several months later, the family moved to a new residence, the sixth change of location since coming to Kumamoto. The dog naturally accompanied them, and before long he had taken a bite out of another stranger. This time, however, the victim was a policeman's wife. Still, Sōseki was not one to cower before authority. The dog, he claimed, had bitten her because she would come early in the morning and dump her garbage in front of the Natsumes' gate. Once again the dog was taken for examination, and once again returned. The next attack, however, left the dog's owner without a defense: one evening, as Sōseki returned from his *utai* lesson, the dog rushed out and pounced on his master, tearing his trousers and the sleeves of his jacket.[22]

Not long after this, Sōseki was pounced upon by the government. What would be the most significant experience of his life appeared out of nowhere, not unlike a dog charging out of the shadows. In 1900 the Japanese government initiated a program to send Japanese overseas to study for a significant period of time; Sōseki and two others were chosen for the pilot program that year. Sōseki himself described the circumstances:

> ... suddenly, after I had been [in Kumamoto] several years, a confidential inquiry came from the Ministry of Education inviting me to go to England for study. At first, I thought of declining. After all, I reasoned, how would it serve the nation for someone like me to go abroad with no clear-cut objective? But my superior who had conveyed the Ministry's inquiry would have none of this. "The Ministry knows why it has chosen you," he said. "There is no need for self-appraisal on your part. Just go." Having no good reason to refuse adamantly, I followed the government's orders and went to England. But sure enough, when I got there, I had nothing to do.[23]

For an individualist like Sōseki, an inquiry that amounted to orders from the government to pack up and go to England with no definite purpose must have been a bitter pill to swallow. He was in no way unattached, holding down a stable job and with a family to support. And that family was growing: by the time he left for London, Kyōko was once again pregnant. One has to consider the possibility that Sōseki was simply unable to come up with a good excuse to dissuade his superiors, though his success at placating the police who were trying to impound his dog makes this seem unlikely. Perhaps he saw the time away from home and family as a chance to clear his head, to rid his mind of its perpetual web of anxieties, and discover some way out of the frustrating maze into which he felt his career had fallen. If such were his hopes for the foreign venture, they were to be abysmally dashed.

Part of the initial problem lay in the fact that his commission from the Ministry of Education was to "study the English language." Of all the individuals involved in English-language education in Japan at that time, Sōseki was perhaps the one who least needed further study. We have already seen what level of accomplishment he had achieved in translation and composition, and contemporary accounts suggest that his ability to speak the language was remarkable. Sōseki was understandably concerned about the nature of the directive, and the summer before his departure from Tokyo he called at the Ministry to discuss the matter. The individual he spoke with, Ueda Mannen, eventually founded the systematic study of Japanese linguistics and was father of one of postwar Japan's most important novelists, Enchi Fumiko. When Sōseki expressed his concerns, he was told that the real purpose of the program was to prepare scholars to teach in university positions that were presently occupied by foreigners. Sōseki had been targeted to replace the popular lecturer Lafcadio Hearn in teaching English literature at Tokyo Imperial University. Thus, it was perfectly acceptable for him to study literature rather than language while in England.[24]

Perhaps relieved that he could take his ongoing struggle with the meaning of foreign literature to the front lines in London, though still somewhat concerned that he had no information on where he was to study, Sōseki began to make preparations for the voyage. The stipend offered him by the Japanese government was paltry by any standards. While it is true that the annual sum of ¥1,800 was a third more than his starting salary at Kumamoto, the expenses of setting up a separate household in London, the cost of attending classes at a university, the outlay for books and tutorials—not to mention any money he might want to send back to help support his family in his absence—make the Ministry's offer seem penurious at best. The allowance for Kyōko and the children was to be a mere ¥300 per year (only three months' worth of his initial Kumamoto high school salary), making the burden even more onerous.

In July of 1900, just two months after receiving official notification of his "selection" by the Ministry of Education, Sōseki gave his last exams at Kumamoto, sold off most of his family's belongings, and took his pregnant wife and their daughter back to Tokyo. They moved into a detached cottage on the property of Kyōko's family, and though this freed them from the need to pay rent, there was still precious little money to take care of domestic needs. As if in omen, not long after they moved in, several members of Kyōko's family, including her mother, came down with dysentery.[25]

On September 8, 1900, Sōseki set sail on the German passenger ship *Preussen* from Yokohama. On board were two other Japanese bound for foreign study; Sōseki was the only one of the three who did not stand at the deck rail to wave goodbye to his family as the ship pulled out. The vessel called at many ports along the way: Kobe, Nagasaki, Shanghai (where, ironically enough, Sōseki met the first man to graduate from the department of English literature at Tokyo Imperial University, now a customs inspector[26]), Hong Kong, Singapore (where he recorded in his English journal: "I put up at a Japanese hotel. There I met a lot of Japanese women who are known technically as 'street-walkers.' Poor abandoned souls! They don't know what they are doing. Driven by penury, they seek shelter in the distant parts of the world, to add ill-fame and infamy to their mother country."[27]), Penang, and Colombo. The trip was not a pleasant one. Sōseki suffered from seasickness and diarrhea, felt ill at ease with Westerners, Western food, Western baths, and Western toilets, and yearned to eat soba noodles and rice mixed with tea. In a diary which contains his shipboard musings, Sōseki recorded the following in English:

The sea is lazily calm and I am dull to the core, lying in my long chair on deck. The leaden sky overhead seems as devoid of life as the dark expanse of waters around, blending their dullness together beyond the distant horizon as if in sympathetic stolidity. While I gaze at them, I gradually lose myself in the lifeless tranquility which surrounds me and seem to grow out of myself on the wings of contemplation to be conveyed to a realm of vision.... Neither heaven nor hell, nor that intermediate stage of human existence which is called by the name of this world, but of vacancy, of nothingness where infinity and eternity seem to swallow one in the oneness of existence, and defies in its vastness any attempts of description. Suddenly the shrill sound of a bell, calling us to lunch, awakened me to the stern reality.... When I am aroused from my reverie my companion at my side jumped up with a long yawning and a very disconsolate face, probably awakened in the midst of a dream in which his wife and children played the most prominent part. Indeed we are 5,000 miles from home, still sailing toward the west as if intent to overtake the fast declining sun or avoid the hot pursuit of the dark night.[28]

En route to England, Sōseki also had the rather peculiar experience of encountering aboard ship an Englishwoman he had met in Kumamoto. Her name was Mrs. Nott, and she was the mother of a Christian lady missionary in Kumamoto. One day, as he sat on deck reading, a foreign voice called out his name. The entries he made in his diary in English suggest some of his reaction to this unexpected meeting.

Here she comes with her Bible under her arm and is waiting for me outside the smoking room where I am engaged in conversation with an American doctor. I rushed out of the room to greet her. Yesterday, she kindly promised to write a letter of introduction for me to Mr. Andrews, Dean of Pembroke College, Cambridge, where I may probably go for study. Her business with me now is to make herself sure of the particular line of study, which I shall take up at the university. She smiles all over her whenever she sees me, which I have seldom noticed in any European ladies, as far as my knowledge goes. Her smiles betray her nature as gentle, so tender, and for aught I know, the fondest of all mothers. Then she is such a charming [talker] too. She never speaks so loud as those vulgar women are sometimes tempted to do. It is true this making her talk somewhat difficult to understand for a novice of the English language like me, especially amidst the din of the steam engines, howling wind and rolling waves. However, her English has such a melody in its intonation that it is a pleasure to listen to her, even when one cannot understand a word of what she says. What is wanted in distinctness, is amply made up by its cadence.

She seems to think that I can understand every word of her, so she never appeals to that way of speaking English which some Englishmen living in Japan are apt to have recourse to, so that their conversation may be easily understand by the natives. But she can never think of adapting her style of conversation to the capacity of her listener at the expense of the grace and elegance of the Queen's English. While word after word flows from her lips in melodious, smooth succession I listen to her half in admiration, half in bewilderment, away she goes like a boat sailing over the languid stillness of the dark glassy surface of the calmest lake. But then the boat goes so fast! If it had not been too rude a thing, I should rather have inclined to compare it to a pony galloping at full speed. Here I catch a word and there another and assisted by some expression on her face, I make a faint attempt to keep pace with her, anxiously waiting for the time when she has had her say. While I am thus engaged in the dubious process of translation on one hand, and cudgel my brains on the other to form an awkward answer, she suddenly pulls up, but alas! only to wheel her horse round to dash through thick and thin in an unbeaten track, leaving me far behind in helpless dismay to overtake her. What an ass of an old boy must I seem in her eyes, gasping, simpering, making now and then a ridiculous attempt to give an answer which is anything but proper.

Now she goes to her promenade deck in full conviction that she has impressed me with due sense of what she has said. Lord bless her! She is such a kind lady for all that.[29]

Sōseki has managed, in the space of a couple of paragraphs written in an alien tongue, to capture precisely the frenetic hail of emotions that pound down upon anyone making those early tentative attempts to understand, and be understood, in a foreign language. His feelings of insecurity about mastering English are perhaps not uncommon for those who choose the study of a foreign language and literature as a career, for such an endeavor of necessity entails a certain division of the personality, a stepping outside oneself to absorb the foreign culture, all the while hoping that one's original identity is resilient enough to stand on its own. There are those inevitable moments when the struggle to master the alien language seems insurmountable, when the entire effort assumes the air of a great fraud because of the unavoidable gaps in cultural and linguistic understanding. Sōseki seems never to have mustered the self-assurance to step into British society. Although the above passage bespeaks his sensitivity to the differences in culture and the difficulties of communicating, it also gives a glimpse of a man who could very possibly have been the center of benignly curious social attention during his stay in England, had he in fact made the effort to become a part of that society.

A month after leaving Yokohama, the ship docked at Aden. Somewhere between there and the first landing in Europe, Sōseki had several discussions with some Christian missionaries. The thoughts he recorded in English about those encounters are revealing of his attitudes toward religion.

> We have on board quite a large number of missionaries, leaving China for England, some on furlough, some owing to the recent disturbances in that country. They never fail to make the most of every opportunity that's offered to make converts of us whom they innocently set down as idolaters.... Those dear souls ... do not hesitate in saying Christ is the incarnation of God.... Is not this, in a sense, an idol-worship? They insist on the idea of one supreme God. Very well. But then does not this idea vary according to different denominations? They say Christianity is the only true religion in the world, but when each denomination holds up its own idea of

the Supreme God as true, it tantamounts to saying that those of other denominations are false and Christianity is the true religion only so far as each denomination is concerned. I have no grudge against Christianity, on the contrary I firmly believe that it is a grand religion, and those who can find faith in it, are surely saved by it. Meanwhile, those whom they call idolaters can likewise find salvation in their way of worship, never so gross, provided they have good faith in them. Religion is after all a matter of faith, not argument or reason. No matter how grand the conception, how deep the reasoning, it is only a toy, splendid to look at, but only waiting to tumble down at the first whip of wind that may happen to blow.... Let people believe in everything which is good and true, in their eyes, and each according to their stage of intellectual development so that they may find therein contentment and happiness. Let my religion be such that it contains every other religion within its transcendental greatness. Let my God be that nothing which is really something, and which I call nothing because, being absolute, it cannot be called by a name involving relativity: which is neither Christ, nor Holy Ghost, nor any other thing, yet at the same time Christ, Holy Ghost and everything.[30]

This treatise is remarkable, as always, for its sophistication of expression, but equally so for the profound engagement with questions of religiosity and the nature of faith to which Sōseki has obviously given considerable thought.

After further brief calls at Naples (where he toured cathedrals, museums, and palaces, and expressed surprise that every roadway in the city was paved) and Genoa, Sōseki took a train to Paris. He remained there a week, visiting the 1900 World's Fair and delighting in its pavilions and exhibitions and marveling at the Paris museums. The "Grand Boulevard" at night, he wrote, was fifty times more splendid than a view of the Ginza on a summer's eve.[31] Similar observations, comparing Japan most unfavorably with what he saw early in his visit to Europe, suggest he was feeling more than a little of the cultural inferiority that was shared by many of his countrymen in the Meiji era.

On the twenty-eighty of October, Sōseki sailed from France to England. Three days later, he did an initial round of sightseeing, taking in the "Tower Bridge, London Bridge, Tower, Monument" during the day, and going with another Japanese to the Haymarket Theatre in the evening to see a performance of Sheridan's *School for Scandal*.[32] But there was pressing business to attend to, namely, finding a school where he could pursue his studies. Armed with the letter of introduction from Mrs. Nott, Sōseki took the train to Cambridge on November 1. He met with the dean of Pembroke College but returned to London the very next day, having abandoned the idea of studying there. On his pension there was no way, he decided, he could afford the kind of life that Cambridge students were living. He later wrote:

> I was inclined to go to either Oxford or Cambridge, since they were centers of learning well-known even to us.... I took the opportunity of going [to Cambridge] to see what sort of place it was.... I met two or three Japanese there. They were all sons and younger brothers of wealthy merchants, who were prepared to spend thousands of yen per year in order to become "gentlemen." My allowance from the government was 1,800 yen a year. In a place where money controlled everything, I could hardly hope to compete with these people.... I thought: my purpose in coming to England is different from that of these easygoing people; I do not know if the gentlemen of England are so impressive as to make it worth my while to imitate them; besides, having already spent my youth in the Orient, why should I now start learning how to conduct myself from these English gentlemen who are younger than I am?[33]

He also considered Edinburgh, but the thick dialect of English spoken there seems to have made him fear that his studies, and perhaps his own spoken language, might suffer.[34] At least in London, once he secured lodgings, he could buy books and go out to see an occasional play.

Lacking an academic base of operations, Sōseki concluded

that the next logical course would be to attend some lectures on English literature at nearby colleges. He sent a letter to Professor William Paton Ker, a specialist in epic and romantic literature and the writings of Tennyson, who was then lecturing at University College, requesting permission to sit in on his lectures. Ker agreed, and Sōseki commuted by "underground railway" to hear what Ker had to say. Unfortunately, Sōseki found the classes as unenlightening as Professor Dixon's had been in Tokyo, so after about two months he stopped attending altogether.

Unable to find a college he could afford, and frustrated by what he perceived as the poor quality of the lectures he attended, Sōseki sought out a third alternative. Late in November he made arrangements for weekly tutorial sessions with W. J. Craig, an eccentric scholar who was one of the editors of the Arden Shakespeare. Craig, who at times seemed to Sōseki more interested in the five shillings per session than in discussing literature, met every Tuesday with his Japanese pupil for a period of somewhat less than a year. The two men discussed English literature, and Craig evaluated some of Sōseki's own attempts at writing in English. On one occasion, Craig remarked that Sōseki's poetry "resembles Blake's, but is incoherent."[35]

Sōseki witnessed the changing of an era while he was in London. In his diary entry for January 23, 1901, he reported in Japanese that Queen Victoria had passed away at 6:30 the previous evening. He continues in English: "Flags are hoisted at half-mast. All the town is in mourning. I, a foreign subject, also wear a black-necktie to show my respectful sympathy. 'The new century has opened rather inauspiciously,' said the shopman of whom I bought a pair of black gloves this morning."[36] On February 2, he accompanied his landlord, Mr. Brett, to observe the funeral procession. Astonished by the size of the crowd at Marble Arch, they continued on to Hyde Park, where, Sōseki notes, "the enormous park was washed by waves of humanity, and every tree in the park was laden with

human fruit." When they reached the street, Sōseki could see
nothing, so Mr. Brett hoisted him onto his shoulders, and he
was able to see the procession pass by "from their waists
up."[37] This experience suggests some of the physical inferiority Sōseki felt while among the "tall and good-looking" people
who were all around him. He laughed at his own face reflected
in a shop window, the figure of a man short and pockmarked,
and regarded himself a "shaggy dog amongst English gentle-
men."[38] On another occasion, as he was strolling around Cam-
berwell, two women noticed him and muttered what Sōseki
took to be the words "least poor Chinese."[39] His own self-con-
sciousness prompted him at times to be depressed, at other
times defensive.

Sōseki changed residences several times during his stay in
England. The people he ended up with as landlords were
largely uninteresting to him, knew nothing of literature, and
struck him as common and ignorant about anything except
their work. Several times his journal records his astonishment
at their primitive assumptions about Japan. "My landlady
commented that if I continued to study so hard, I would become a fabulously wealthy man when I returned to Japan. I
had a good laugh."[40]

Sōseki's earnest quest for an understanding of English literature impelled him to reject virtually every other activity.
His rather sparse diary of his London days suggests that most
of his time was spent buying and studying used books, reading and replying to letters from family and friends, and perus-
ing Japanese magazines sent from home. He shunned society,
admitting the possibility that there might be "some little
value" in associating with other students, visiting libraries, attending public debates, and hobnobbing with professors, but
concluded that such activities would waste precious money
and make his stay pass all too quickly.[41] He was unable to
overcome his anxiety over the paltry amount of money he was
receiving from the Japanese government. His monetary concerns, together with his fear that he would never be able to

master his subject and his dislike of British food ("The food at
my lodgings is highly unpalatable. Until recently several
Japanese had been staying there, so it was a bit better, but recently it has gotten worse and worse. But I can't be too picky
when I'm only paying 25 shillings a week, and the family, unfortunately, seems to be hard pressed for money."[42]), took
their toll on his physical and mental health. "If I don't walk
the entire day, my stomach bothers me; if I go out walking, I
always end up spending about two yen before I get back
home. What a dilemma!"[43] By the end of February, he was beginning to shell out money to buy mineral water from Carls-
bad, which was supposed to relieve stomach distress. Every
account of his life notes that, to all intents and purposes, Sōseki's entire two years in England were spent cloistered in his
room, reading books and convincing himself beyond question
that an unscalable wall separated him from the literature he
was examining.

The misery which Sōseki endured for over two years in
London was largely self-imposed. It is not hard to imagine
someone with Sōseki's intelligence, sensitivity, and fluency
with language (excepting exceedingly minor errors) becoming
something of a cultural phenomenon in London. Not that he
would have welcomed being looked upon as an exotic curiosity, but even at its worst such treatment would have been vastly superior to the virtual exile which he inflicted on himself.
One need only compare Sōseki's wretched isolation in England with the experience of his literary contemporary, Mori
Ōgai, who lived in Germany between 1884–89. Ōgai was out-
going and gregarious, eager to associate with the German people and absorb all that he could of the language, culture, literature, and philosophy of the West. Accounts of Ōgai's stay in
Germany are filled with visits to the theater and opera, attendance at dance parties and soirees. He even managed to find
the time to squeeze in an affair with a young German dancing
girl. For all that, Ōgai also accomplished his (admittedly
clear-cut, in contrast to Sōseki's) primary mission as a doctor:

namely, to study Western techniques of medical hygiene.[44] Yet he also returned to Japan to introduce European literary concepts such as romanticism and naturalism, to translate the poetry of Goethe and Byron, the plays of Ibsen, the serious fiction of Hans Christian Andersen, and to launch a significant literary career of his own. It is tempting to wonder how different Sōseki's overseas experience might have been, and how different its impact on his later career might have turned out, had he been more capable of extending himself to join the society that surrounded him.

Except for a few Japanese associates with whom he occasionally went out or sat in conversation, Sōseki ventured out infrequently. In February of 1902 he felt compelled to attend a tea held in Dulwich by a Mrs. Edghill. He set out unwillingly in a gentle snowstorm, only to find himself at his destination thirty minutes before the appointed hour. By then, the snow was falling fiercely. Convinced that decorum would not allow him to call until the proper time, he wandered about in the snow for half an hour, fashioning it a "snow-viewing." When he was finally shown into the drawing room of the house, he was surprised to find half a dozen English ladies there. "There were unfamiliar women to the right of me, unfamiliar women to the left of me. Even the lady of the house was unknown to me. I thought her senseless to invite to an 'at home' a foreigner, and a Japanese at that, whom she had never met before, but nothing could be done about it. And I suppose she had invited me out of a sense of duty, and I had come out of a sense of duty.... It was a total waste of time. Western society is absurd. Who created such a stifling society? And what is there of interest about it?"[45]

Sōseki's second, and essentially final, diffident sally into British society took place just two months later, again to a tea in Dulwich. There his hostess, Mrs. Edghill, and his acquaintance from Kumamoto, Mrs. Nott, lectured him on the virtues of Christianity. "Left with no recourse," he confesses to his journal, "I told them my feelings on the subject. Mrs. Edghill asked me if I had any desire to pray. I told her I could not conceive of any being to whom I should pray. Mrs. E., saying how pitiful it was that I did not know this great comfort, wept. It was pathetic. Mrs. E. said she would pray for me, and I thanked her. Then she asked if I would promise her one thing, and when I told her I would promise because she was so kind as to be concerned for me, she told me I must read the Gospels in the Bible. I felt sorry for her, so I said I would read it. When I was leaving, she reminded me not to forget my promise, and I told her I most certainly would not. So now I have to read the Gospels."[46] It might be worth noting here that nowhere in his subsequent diary entries does Sōseki comment that he either has or has not fulfilled his promise.

Sōseki's second daughter was born on January 27 of that year; a friend wrote him of the event the following day. Perhaps because he had changed lodgings twice already since arriving in London, or perhaps because the postal service between England and Japan was still in its infancy, the letter reached Sōseki on March 13.

That spring Sōseki made a friend—a Japanese scientist named Ikeda who had studied in Berlin and who would stay with Sōseki in London for two months. Their conversations stimulated Sōseki to continue his studies on a more formal, rational basis, and at Ikeda's prompting he hit upon the idea of producing his own "theory of literature," something uniquely his own, not a definition borrowed from abroad. It was this notion that ultimately led Sōseki to seclude himself in his room, reading voraciously and taking copious notes that would eventually be published as his *Bungaku-ron* (Theory of Literature) in 1907. Ironically, this new intellectual window, which appeared amidst his despair over understanding literature, would also lead him toward the portals of madness. His utter isolation while he pursued his "theory of literature" all but tore him loose from the moorings that tied him to other human beings, and in his search to comprehend what literature had to say about the human condition, he came perilously close to sacrificing his own humanity. At one point he reached the conclusion that the study of literary works themselves would never lead him to his goal, that in fact he needed to have a broader understanding of human society itself. His reading shifted to works on science, psychology, philosophy, and other fields in his search for the key to understanding.

Sōseki later described this difficult period as a life lived trapped inside a sack. In a 1914 lecture to university students, he said:

> I worked hard. I strove to accomplish something. But none of the books I read helped me tear through the sack. I could search from one end of London to the other, I felt, and never find what I needed. I stayed in my room, thinking how absurd this all was. No amount of reading was going to fill this emptiness in the pit of my stomach. And when I resigned myself to the hopelessness of my task, I could no longer see any point to my reading books.
>
> It was then that I realized that my only hope for salvation lay in fashioning for myself a conception of what literature is, working from the ground up and relying on nothing but my own efforts.... My next step was to strengthen—perhaps I should say to build anew—the foundations on which I stood in my study of literature. For this, I began to read books that had nothing to do with literature. If, before, I had been dependent on others, if I had been other-centered, it occurred to me now that I must become self-centered. I became absorbed in scientific studies, philosophical speculation, anything that would support this position.... Self-centeredness became for me a new beginning, I confess, and it helped me to find what I thought would be my life's work. I resolved to write books, to tell people that they need not imitate Westerners, that running blindly after others as they were doing would only cause them great anxiety....
>
> My anxiety disappeared without a trace. I looked out on London's gloom with a happy heart. I felt that after years of agony my pick had at last struck a vein of ore. A ray of light had broken through the fog and illuminated the way I must take.
>
> At the time that I experienced this enlightenment, I had

been in England for more than a year. There was no hope of my accomplishing the task I had set for myself while I was in a foreign country. I decided to collect all the materials I could find and to complete my work after returning to Japan.[47]

Twelve years after the fact, Sōseki may have felt he had attained a sense of relief at reaching this conclusion. Yet around the time Ikeda left London, Sōseki was recording in his diary, "Recently I have been very unhappy. The most trivial things irritate me. I wonder if I have some nervous disorder. On the other hand I feel extremely audacious. It is very peculiar."[48] By September of 1902 his mental condition had so deteriorated that other Japanese studying in London passed rumors on to the Ministry of Education that Sōseki was mad.

It is the consensus among those who have studied Sōseki's life that he did in fact suffer something like a nervous breakdown toward the end of his stay in England. When he was reprimanded by the Ministry of Education for not sending in a required report on the progress of his studies, Sōseki sent them a blank sheet of paper, suggesting the depth of his despair over his research.[49] He was encouraged by those around him to seek some relief from his constant studying, to take up bicycle riding or to travel. He took their advice, and perhaps was making some progress, but shortly before his return to Japan at the end of 1902, he received news that must have wounded him deeply. His closest literary comrade, Masaoka Shiki—the man who had sparked his interest in haiku and fostered his earliest writings—had died. On December 5, Sōseki left London and began the trip back to Japan.

It would be extreme to suggest that Sōseki returned to Japan a broken man. He was, after all, only a year away from beginning his extraordinary career as a novelist. But it would be fair to say that, emotionally and physically, he would never again be the same. Though he had periods of peace over the remaining fourteen years of his life, and though he was not constantly racked with pain, the recurrence of mental imbalance and intense stomach pains from his ulcers never afforded him long periods of ease. It is almost as though, in seeking to tear himself free from foreign definitions of culture and literature, which he knew could only be of limited use in his attempt to create a modern Japanese literature, Sōseki ruptured something within his own body and mind. And perhaps it is in that struggle—the ambivalent effort to absorb foreign culture while yet rejecting it as the ultimate solution to native problems of definition—that Japanese today continue to see glimpses of their nation's struggle toward modernity in the Meiji period, a struggle that in many ways continues to this very day.

Whatever Sōseki's inner anguish might have been upon his return, there were countless honors awaiting him. In April of 1903 he was appointed lecturer at the First High School and took over the lectureship in English literature at Tokyo Imperial University from Lafcadio Hearn. Hearn had been a popular teacher among his students, and he was a difficult act to follow. Sōseki made diligent efforts to teach theories of form in English literature and conducted a class which focused on the reading and translation of *Silas Marner*, but neither course captured the imagination of his wary students. The following year he altered his approach to include considerations of *Macbeth* and other Shakespeare plays, which had a much better reception.

Sōseki also had difficulty readjusting to family life. Having been isolated, virtually hermetic, for so long, the tensions between himself and his wife and two daughters must have been uncommonly painful. The pendulum of his mental stability continued to swing so erratically that Kyōko took the girls and returned to live with her parents for a period of two months, waiting for him to restore his balance of mind. They reconciled, however, before Kyōko gave birth to a third daughter in October. Sōseki's associates reported that he was also displaying signs of paranoia, convinced as he was that he was being tailed by detectives. The shift from living a solitary life abroad to everyday life in Tokyo appears to have exacerbated his mental problems.

In an effort to provide Sōseki with some beneficial mental activity, the editor of *Hototogisu*, Sōseki's old friend Taka-hama Kyoshi, worked with him on the composition of some poetry, and finally persuaded Sōseki to produce a work of prose. Sōseki wrote what he intended as a short story, titled "*Wagahai wa neko de aru*" (I Am a Cat). The story was so well received when Kyoshi read it aloud to a gathering of Shiki's disciples, and later when it appeared in the January 1905 issue of the journal, that Sōseki had no choice but to continue serializing new chapters of the cat's adventures. As Kyoshi had hoped, the popular reception of the work did much to soothe Sōseki's nerves and restore his equilibrium— for a time, at least.

The reading public's enthusiasm for *I Am a Cat*—which, as many commentators have noted, is less a novel than a se-ries of wry observations about the shortcomings of contempo-rary Japanese intellectuals, observations which Sōseki was su-perbly qualified to make from his perspective as a recent returnee from overseas—strengthened Sōseki's desire to free himself of the burden of teaching so that he could devote him-self exclusively to writing. He had taken on a third teaching position, and was growing increasingly restive. In 1905 he wrote:

> My time is wasted every day over visitors. On reflection, I've come to remember that I ought not to be doing this until my death. It is going against nature unreasonably to try to do so many things at once—teaching at three different schools, receiving so many guests and visitors, studying freely for my-self, and doing creative work as well. I'm essentially a man of few wants who will be content if I am able to write during my whole life two or three works that will seem satisfactory to myself; if this is possible, I don't care in the least about other things. But to do that I've got to eat beef and eggs, and be-cause of such a requisite, it has come about that I have been forgetting my own nature in that I am following, to my infi-nite regret, a profession against my will. (This sounds ridicu-

lous, doesn't it?) Anyway, what I want to quit is teaching, and what I desire to do is creative work.[50]

He was certainly stretching himself thin, for in addition to his teaching and his meetings with all manner of people, he was beginning to attract a group of loyal literary disciples, and his creative activities proceeded apace. In 1905 he published several stories drawn from his overseas experience, including "Tower of London" and "The Carlyle Museum" set in London, and two stories that take place in medieval England. And of course there was no relief from family duties: a fourth daughter was born that winter.

Before the last installment of *I Am a Cat* was completed, Sōseki had started on his second novel, *Botchan*. As mentioned earlier, it is a fully fictionalized account of his year of teaching in Matsuyama. The title character is one of the most memorable creations in modern Japanese fiction, a rigid individualist given to making snap judgments of others and impatient with their mistakes. Botchan is remarkable because he is both an appealing portrait of the brash, utterly unabashed *Edokko*, or "child of Edo" (so unlike the typical stereotype of the "shy, polite Japanese"), and also a compelling study of overweening individualism carried to an extreme. There can be no doubt that Sōseki found something appealing in Botchan's outspoken, self-assertive manner, but one can also detect a thoughtful reflection on individual behavior that begins to intrude upon the rights of others. At the end of the novel *Botchan* may feel he has achieved a moral victory when he gives the hypocritical principal a thrashing, but as a result he has to resign his position and begin working as a traincar mechanic back in Tokyo, while still under the protective wing of his adoring maid, Okiyo. The individualism that Sōseki presents in this early novel is a peculiar mixture of juvenile stubbornness, intolerance, and admirable self-assertiveness. This early, amusing portrait of a modern, rebellious individual is a prelude to the deeper consideration he will give the topic in later works. For all his flaws there is much to love and be amused at in Botchan, and Japanese readers continue to do both.

In the space of two weeks that same year, Sōseki produced *Kusamakura* (The Three-Cornered World), which he described as a "haiku-like" novel. Whatever Sōseki learned from his studies of the forms of Western literature, he was determined not to be caught in the trap of formal repetitiveness himself. His quest for a literary form that was a true representation of himself and his country made him into a roving technician. It is safe to say that Sōseki never repeated the same formal structure in his novels. While there is much similarity in imagery, in the patterns of triangular relationships, in the motifs of betrayal and ambivalence in his works, the range of novelistic forms that Sōseki employs to examine these themes is truly impressive.

The Three-Cornered World is perhaps most easily described as an attempt to sketch life free of its emotional entanglements. In this sense, it bears much in common with the practice of *shasei*—of drawing objective pictures from life—that Masaoka Shiki, his poet friend, had attempted in his haiku. And yet, by the end of the work, the ideal aesthetic world which the characters have sought to create through withholding their emotions is shattered when Nami catches a glimpse of her ex-husband and a look of compassion flickers across her face. It is in that moment of betrayal—of emotions forcing their way to the surface unbidden—that the artist finds, to his surprise, the picture he always wanted to paint.

Toward the end of 1906, a group of Sōseki's disciples began meeting at his home every Thursday at 3:00 P.M. to discuss literature. Their gathering later took on the name Mokuyō-kai (The Thursday Group), and their circle came to include writers from many different persuasions who were attracted to Sōseki for a variety of reasons. The Thursday Group meetings were perhaps the most important forums for the discussion of literature in pre-war Japan.

Sōseki's growing popularity made him the target of several seductive offers. Two prestigious academic positions were offered, and the *Yomiuri Shinbun*, one of Tokyo's most powerful newspapers, extended an invitation to take charge of their literary column. Sōseki rejected them all. Then, just as he had confounded his friends and colleagues twelve years earlier by resigning from two solid teaching posts in Tokyo to head for the hinterlands, so again in 1907 Sōseki caused the pompous pundits of his day to scratch their heads in disbelief when he announced in print that he would be leaving his prestigious teaching jobs and taking employment with the *Asahi Shinbun*, the leading daily newspaper in Japan. Sōseki defended this decision with the simple remark, "If being a newspaperman is a trade, then being a university-man is also a trade."[51]

His duties at the *Asahi*, for which he was paid ¥200 a month, included writing at least one novel a year for serialization, agreeing not to publish fiction outside of the *Asahi*, and doing no writing of any sort for other papers. Public response to the announcement was remarkable: shortly after the paper advertised that Sōseki would soon begin publishing a novel titled *Gubijinsō* (The Poppy), Mitsukoshi Department Store started selling yukatas with poppy designs. Other stores hawked "poppy rings," and paperboys at train stations called out "Read Sōseki's Poppy!"[52]

Shortly after he completed *The Poppy*, Sōseki's first son was born. His own mental condition had improved, but the trade-off between his mind and his body continued: no sooner had his nerves settled than his stomach began to trouble him. This pattern continued until his death nine years later.

In November of 1907, a man who had worked as a miner joined the Sōseki household. The story of his life Sōseki transformed into the novel *Kōfu* (The Miner), which he finished by January of the following year. This was followed by the works that are usually described as belonging to Sōseki's "middle period," highlighted by the trilogy of novels comprising *Sanshirō* (1908), *Sorekara* (And Then, 1909), and *Mon*

(The Gate, 1910). The gradual darkening of Sōseki's view of human relationships, which reaches its peak in *Kokoro* of 1914, can be traced through the volumes of this trilogy. In one way or another, each of the three works deals with individuals who suffer because they are unable to share their innermost feelings with others. A love triangle, explicit or implied, lies at the center of each work, but the betrayal of honest emotion leads to isolation and frustrated silence. Sanshirō, the hero of the first volume, comes from the countryside to study in Tokyo, still full of youthful optimism. His experiences there, particularly his inability to express his true feelings for a woman he has come to love, turn him toward the bleaker disillusionment that casts its shadow over the later novels. In *And Then*, the hero Daisuke tries to put things back into their "natural" order—he asks his old friend Hiraoka to give up his wife, with whom Daisuke had long ago fallen in love. The problem with his life, and with all of Japanese society, Daisuke has concluded, is that the proper order of "nature" has been disrupted by people not following their true inclinations. And he is setting out to restore a natural order to the world. The conclusion of the novel finds him sitting on a streetcar with his head spinning, emotionally overwrought and out of control. It would appear that the feeble efforts of one man—too late and too calculated—cannot set to rights a cynical world. The tone in *The Gate*, the third volume in the "trilogy," is one of muted suffering. The vigor and optimism of Sanshirō's youthfulness are transmuted into the quiet despair of a middle-aged couple: not even the search for religious enlightenment helps them cope with their loneliness.

In September of 1908, the cat which had been the model for Sōseki's first novel died, and the author sent death notices to his friends. A second son was born to him at the end of that year. Another literary product of that year was the collection of psychoanalytically interesting stories, *Yume-jūya* (Ten Nights of Dream). Between March and November of 1909, Sōseki had to cope with visits from his foster father, Shiobara, whom he had not seen for many years. Shiobara, learning that his former adopted son was now a popular author, came to seek financial support. Sōseki would describe the painful opening of old wounds in his penultimate novel, and his only truly autobiographical work, *Michikusa* (Grass on the Wayside, 1915). In November of 1909, Sōseki founded the literary column for the *Asahi* newspaper. Because he was fervently opposed to the mainstream trend of self-absorbed, confessional autobiographical "fiction" that was sweeping over the Japanese literary landscape, the *Asahi* column was regarded as something of a bastion of anti-naturalism. Still, Sōseki proved himself to be an open-minded, non-partisan editor, and both allowed publication of writings by "I-novelists" in the *Asahi* and praised those of literary merit.

Sōseki's health began to deteriorate significantly in 1910. He wrote *The Gate* while enduring severe stomach pain, and spent over a month in the hospital that summer for treatment of his ulcer. From there he retired to an inn at Shuzenji hot springs to recuperate, but his condition worsened and soon he vomited an alarming amount of blood. The doctors were ready to give up hope, but he improved gradually and was eventually able to return to the hospital, where he remained until February of 1911. During this trying time, Sōseki sought to sustain his spirits by once again composing *kanshi* (a common practice for him in times of severe stress) and haiku as well, and he also took up painting in order to settle his nerves.

By June of 1911 he had recovered sufficiently to take on the rigors of a lecture tour, but once again ulcers felled him away from home, and he was hospitalized in Osaka. He returned to Tokyo only to require hemorrhoidal surgery, which necessitated regular visits to the clinic until the spring of the following year. His condition was not helped by the news brought to him in November of 1911: his fifth and last daughter, Hinako, born in March of 1910, had unexpectedly and inexplicably died. It came as a major blow to Sōseki; in December he wrote: "My stomach has cracked. My mind, too, it

Sōseki in 1912.

Marriage interview (*miai*) photograph of Nakane Kyōko (later Mrs. Natsume Sōseki), 1895.

Graduating class of Fifth High School, Kumamoto (Sōseki middle row, second from right).

Sōseki, daughter Fudeko, and Matsune Tōyōjō (haiku disciple) around time *The Gate* was completed, 1910.

Commemorative photo of Sōseki party at Shuzenji hot springs, 1911.

Sōseki in 1912.

Sōseki at writing desk around time of *Inside My Glass Doors*, 1914.

seems, for I feel an incurable sorrow each time I recall [the loss of my child]."[53]

Amid all his personal suffering, Sōseki continued to wage his battles against the world of hypocritical bureaucrats and the tendency of Japanese to ape the West. In February of 1911, the Ministry of Education, perhaps wishing to capitalize on their own sagacity at selecting a future famous novelist for a fellowship to England, tried to offer Sōseki an honorary Doctor of Letters degree. Sōseki angrily declined, affronted by any recognition from officialdom. In fact, he blustered, it was impudent of the government to even consider giving him a degree without asking him first whether he cared to have it.[54] In the same vein, Sōseki posed what would become a classic argument about the flaws inherent in Japan's attempts at modernization in a series of public lectures, which made him extremely popular in many parts of Japan (much along the lines of Twain or Dickens). While acknowledging that Japan had made tremendous technological and intellectual strides in a short span of time, he asserted that all such progress was only on the surface; that his countrymen, in their scramble to play catch-up with the West, had utterly ignored the moral foundations of Western culture; and, in a telling projection of his own personal dilemma, Sōseki suggested that the strains of coping with the rapidity and intensity of modernization had emotionally crippled the Japanese people, leading them to suffer from "national nervous prostration."[55]

The trilogy of Sōseki's "mature years" began in 1912 with the completion of *Higan sugi made* (To the Spring Equinox and Beyond; trans. 1985), progressed through *Kōjin* (The Wayfarer, 1913; trans. 1967), and concluded with his finest literary achievement, *Kokoro*. The deeper maturity of *Kokoro* certainly owes something to one of the major spiritual crises in Japan in the early part of the century: the death of the Emperor Meiji on July 30, 1912. That event provides an important coda to Sōseki's novel, suggesting both the end of an era for Japan and the end of a miserable life for Sensei, a man who cannot cope with the pain that his selfish mistakes have brought on himself and others. There is certainly something of Sōseki in this characterization: just as Sensei sealed off the borders to his own heart from his wife, Sōseki likewise allowed his paranoiac fear of others to taint his marriage, turning his back on Kyōko for a series of minor infractions around the time he wrote *Kokoro*.[56]

Most likely it is no coincidence that *Kokoro* explores the darkest corners of the human heart—the corners that are exposed to light when individualism is distorted by human avarice—by setting up traditional patterns of interpersonal relationships and then examining how each of those relationships is destroyed by betrayal. The pattern which Sōseki employs in the novel is the age-old Confucian model based upon filial piety: the relationships between lord and vassal; father and son; husband and wife; elder and younger; friend and friend. There are key examples of each in *Kokoro*, and each is characterized in the modern period by treachery. The elder–younger pattern is perhaps most clearly represented by the relationship between Sensei and the young student narrator of the novel's first part. The bond that is established between these two paradigmatic characters (each of them is given only a role name, not a personal name) seems to be the strongest, most enduring in the novel. In many ways the student is a Sensei-in-training, which is often interpreted to mean that he will learn from Sensei's example and avoid the pitfalls of betrayal. Yet, as the novel closes with Sensei's testament, we as readers are left up in the air. We do not learn what impact the story of Sensei's life has had on the student; all we know is that he has abandoned his own father in the countryside (thereby destroying another conventional bond of filiality) so that he can race futilely toward the modern Tokyo where Sensei, his intellectual father (transforming the relationship into a Confucian father–son association), already lies dead from suicide. We must speculate without guidance from Sōseki on how the experience will affect the young man's life.

Will he be disowned by his family for leaving them at the moment of his father's death? Will he keep the secret entrusted him by Sensei and honor Sensei's dying request that he never reveal the tale to Sensei's wife? (The text includes a subtle suggestion that he does not keep this trust: early in the story the student notes that Sensei's wife is still alive; yet at the very end, Sensei's final request is that the student not tell this story until she, too, is dead.) And, of course, Sensei himself plays less than fair in his relationship with his wife by sealing off the doors of communication and refusing to share the sources of his terminal pain.

The core of Sensei's agony lies, of course, in a betrayal of the relationship between friend and friend, yet another of the Confucian patterns. And the cycle of duplicity is completed toward the end of the novel, when the betrayal of the Emperor Meiji by General Nogi is atoned for after Meiji's death by Nogi's suicide. This becomes an example for Sensei's own decision to take his life.

Sōseki's tortured attitudes toward human relations in the modern period come through vividly in this novel. *Kokoro* is clearly not a reactionary argument for a return to old-fashioned Chinese models of human interaction. At the same time, however, in a typically ambivalent manner, Sōseki makes use of these Confucian models to suggest the various ways in which unbridled individualistic behavior can destroy virtually every relationship in a person's life. By ending the novel inconclusively, forcing the reader to determine what lies ahead for the student narrator, Sōseki is simultaneously compelling us to determine the consequences of our own acts of disloyalty. *Kokoro*, having posed the problem of utter human isolation after all ties have been severed, ends not with a didactic solution to the dilemma, but with a grim question mark.

Kokoro was completed in August of 1914. For the next two months Sōseki retired to his bed with another ulcer attack, then in November gave his best-known public lecture, "*Watakushi no kojin-shugi*" (My Individualism), to a group of students at the elite Gakushūin University. It is a memorable address, filled with personal reminiscences and some truly insightful thoughts on the pleasures and pains of being an individual in modern society. Sōseki told the students:

> … unless a man has attained some degree of ethical culture, there is no value in his developing his individuality, no value in his using his power or wealth…. When a man is devoid of character, everything he does presents a threat. When he seeks to develop his individuality without restraints, he obstructs others; when he attempts to use power, he merely abuses it; when he tries to use money, he corrupts society. Someday you will be in a position where you can do all of these things quite easily. That is why you must not fail to become upstanding men of character….
>
> I simply believe that freedom without a sense of duty is not true freedom, for such self-indulgent freedom cannot exist in society. And if, for a moment, it did, it would quickly be expelled, stamped out by others. I sincerely wish for all of you to be free. At the same time I want to make very certain that you understand what is meant by duty….
>
> … the development of your individuality will have a great bearing on your happiness. Thus it would seem to me that we must keep for ourselves and grant to others a degree of liberty such that I can turn left while you turn right, each of us equally unhindered so long as what we do has no effect on others. This is what I mean when I speak of individualism….
>
> More simply stated, individualism is a philosophy that replaces cliquism with values based on personal judgment of right and wrong. An individualist is not forever running with the group, forming cliques that thrash around blindly in the interests of power and money. That is why there lurks beneath the surface of his philosophy a loneliness unknown to others. As soon as we deny our little groups, then I simply go my way and I let the other man go his, unhindered. Sometimes, in some instances, we cannot avoid becoming scattered. That is what is lonely.[57]

Forced by ill health to remain at home, Sōseki took advantage of the enforced leisure to record his musings and recount visits from a variety of people in a revealing personal document titled *Garasudo no naka* (Inside My Glass Doors), published in early 1915. It is tempting to concoct a metaphor based on an image of Sōseki at this point in his life, nearing the end of a brief but extraordinary literary career, seated almost motionless behind the glass doors of his home, receiving admiring visitors and pondering the death of his cat and other matters of consequence, while he suffers miserably from his badly ulcerated stomach. That immobile, inwardly anguished portrait bears much in common with the fictional characters Sōseki created, and with the struggles of the country in which he lived.

That March and April he took a trip to Kyoto with friends, but a fifth ulcer attack led to his wife being summoned to Kyoto by telegram. Perhaps it was ultimately a sense of his own tenuous mortality which, that spring, led Sōseki to begin composing his only autobiographical novel, *Grass on the Wayside*. At the end of that year, several talented young authors joined the Thursday Group, including Akutagawa Ryūnosuke, perhaps the greatest short story writer of Japan's modern period, and Kume Masao. The advent of these writers helped to bolster Sōseki's spirits. As always, he was a generous mentor. To a large extent, it was Sōseki's praise of one of Akutagawa's first stories, *"Hana"* (The Nose, 1915), that brought the young writer to the attention of the literary world.

Severe pain in his arms forced Sōseki to abandon a piece he started writing early in 1916. He went to Yugawara hot springs to receive therapy for rheumatism, but was soon diagnosed as having diabetes. While undergoing treatment for that ailment, he began his last, unfinished novel, *Meian* (Light and Darkness, 1916; trans. 1971). He would work on the novel in the mornings, then devote his afternoons to mental and physical therapy by painting, practicing calligraphy, and composing *kanshi*. This proved to be his most productive period of writing Chinese poetry. One of the last *kanshi* he composed goes as follows:

When I lose heaven, I lose my simplicity.
When I think I have found the way, it distances itself
    from me.
Human wisdom brings with it death;
In the world of goblins the righteous are emaciated.
When hurled onto the earth it resounds splendidly,
    the gold-inlaid sword;
When hurled into the sky it radiates brilliantly:
    the golden orb of night,
But I trudge along the road, alone, swallowing my tears,
My parents both gone, I stand bewildered at the broad
    crossroads.[58]

Some critics have suggested that there are Zen overtones in Sōseki's final poetry; others that the dominant philosophical stance late in his life can be characterized by what his disciples called *sokuten kyoshi* (to forsake the self and follow Heaven). Much has been written about this abstract motto, probing the irony that a man so dedicated to the pursuit of individualism should conclude that only through liberation from egotistical concerns and the focusing upon loftier goals could one find true peace.[59]

On November 22, 1916, Sōseki had his final major ulcer attack. Ten days later there was massive internal hemorrhaging, and on the ninth of December he died. The newspaper obituaries were longer and professed a greater sense of national loss than those for an army general who died at the same time.[60]

An Infatuation with Modernity
Tanizaki Jun'ichirō

There is virtually no chance, it seems safe to venture, that the likeness of Tanizaki Jun'ichirō will ever appear on any denomination of Japanese currency....

One sure-fire way to measure the gap in cultural understanding between Japan and the West is to mention the name "Tanizaki Jun'ichirō" to a Japanese. Unsuspecting American college students who have received basic training in modern Japanese literature at any of the premier institutions in the United States will surely go to Japan convinced, either from the persuasive force of their professors' lectures or from the sheer bulk of *The Makioka Sisters*, that Tanizaki was the greatest Japanese novelist of the twentieth century.

When a student so convinced engages a Japanese in conversation about literature, the inevitable question will surface: "Who is your favorite Japanese writer?" There are few better ways to elicit looks of amazement and disbelief from "typical" Japanese than to answer "Tanizaki." Some, in fact, express dismay that Tanizaki is even mentioned in a course on modern literature. (A few of these people will have heard comments by two prominent Japanese critics to the effect that Tanizaki was utterly lacking in intellectual substance.[1]) One can almost detect a shade of embarrassment that a foreigner has come into contact with the side of Japanese life that Tanizaki relished depicting. It could, after all, be argued that an obsessive concern with "lust, cleptomania, sado-masochism, homosexuality, foot-fetishism, coprophilia, and Eisen-bahnkrankheit (railroad phobia)"[2] does not constitute a focus upon the concerns of the average citizen. In a culture as meticulous in its definitions of acceptable social behavior and as uncomfortable with deviations as Japan's, the extremes that take center stage in Tanizaki's writings are bound to raise eyebrows and blood pressure levels, and the impertinent suggestion from a foreign reader that such a deviant may represent the finest that Japan has to offer in modern literature can cause appreciable consternation. Add to this the fact that Tanizaki's life could be considered a veritable model of aberrant behavior in Japanese society, and it becomes clear why questions remain in the contemporary Japanese mind about his status both as an artist and as a human being.[3]

With a few prime exceptions, many of Tanizaki's earliest works are indeed loathsome in content, no matter how exquisitely framed as literary art. Similarly, the abject groveling of Tanizaki's many heroes at the feet of icily cruel beauties, when taken only in its most literal sense, can be difficult for many readers to relate to on a personal level. Never mind that Tanizaki was suggesting, by exposing his own private fetishes, that we all have dark corners in our psychic makeup, shadowy recesses in our innermost minds packed with unfulfilled—and often unfulfillable—dreams that run counter to what we expect of ourselves, and most certainly counter to what others expect of us; and yet these dreams often shape who and what we inwardly are, irrespective of our outward selves. That fundamental vision (not, it might be worth noting, totally alien to the vision of human deceitfulness that Sōseki displayed in works like *Kokoro*) is an unsettling one, and in our nominations for "great writers" we often make the most comfortable choices. *Huckleberry Finn* we can regard as the great American novel only after sufficient time has passed to allow us to feign that racism is no longer an issue of personal relevance.

And what of the key relationships and yearnings in Tanizaki's fiction? Leading Western scholars of Tanizaki have argued that "the typical Tanizaki 'hero' is the Eternal Child in
pursuit of Eternal Mother,"[4] and suggest very persuasively
that the pursuit is essentially an incestuous one. This is fundamentally a "Genji complex,"[5] a lifelong search for a mother
figure who can both restore the wholeness of childhood and
satisfy the passions of adulthood. A prominent Japanese critic
proposed, "He might be said in one sense to have spent his
whole life as a child; nostalgia for childhood is a basic motif
in his art."[6] There can be no question that Tanizaki's formative years played a major role in shaping his psychological
and artistic tastes, and that he continued throughout his life to
be preoccupied with the games and fantasies of youth. How
else to explain him sitting down many times during his career—and in the greatest detail at age sixty-nine—to write so
fondly and ardently of those days?

Here again, the common man is very likely not going to
see any immediate, direct connection between his own personal experiences of childhood and the incestuous fantasies
played out time and again in Tanizaki's fiction.[7] Problems inevitably arise when a reader looks only at the "story" of a
work of literature and ignores the larger, vastly more important task of allowing the mind to make a metaphor of the fiction so that it speaks to us on the generalized level of common
human experience. As we proceed through the morass of
Tanizaki's life, we can, if we so choose, pause occasionally to
take a voyeur's pleasure from various peculiarities in his love
life; but it is far more important in working our way through
his fiction to do so as intelligent readers, letting our minds
make something more of the fetishes and foibles contained
therein. A reader unwilling to plunge into the shadows rife in
Tanizaki's stories will exit them unenlightened about anything
other than one specific man's private quirks. Those who will
make the effort to linger in the shadows themselves, setting
their own psyches free to wander for a time, will discover
there something about themselves as well.

In short, then, the relationship that Tanizaki obliges us as readers to assume with him is ultimately a subordinate, masochistic one. He is still playing the games of childhood when he narrates a tale to us, and he insists that we put on a blindfold and allow him to guide us through the dark. He will lead us wherever his imagination suggests, and sometimes the corridors will be filled with abhorrent images. But if we choose not to submit, not to turn our own imaginations over to Tanizaki's guidance, the journey through the catacombs will not be one of discovery, but merely of discomfort.

Much of what reoccurs in Tanizaki's life and works is a study in the nature and power of infatuation. The standard view of him as a writer who reveled in modernity until after the 1923 earthquake, when the move to Kansai put him in touch with traditional Japan, is certainly accurate enough, and useful in dividing up stages of his experience and literary career. But it is equally important to recognize that much of his personal experience—ranging from his capricious selection and deselection of women to his tastes in food, his aesthetic and literary preferences, his fondness even for certain types of toilet facilities—seems to have been motivated by a variety of fleeting infatuation that swept over him like waves of passion, only to leave him unsatisfied once they had subsided. His early, playful fiction can be regarded as a means to regenerate the obsession, to keep the infatuation alive long enough to derive pleasure from it. And the many tangled twists in his love life can be traced to the same thirst for uninterrupted stimulation. It is only when his romantic life and the inspiration for his fiction are united in the figure of his third wife, Matsuko, that Tanizaki is finally able to put infatuation behind him and devote himself exclusively and intimately to the creation of an idealized world of traditional values in the masterworks of his late career. The meanderings of his life, then, are what will engage us in the pages ahead.

✳ ✳ ✳

Tanizaki Jun'ichirō was born in the Nihonbashi section of Tokyo on the twenty-fourth of July in 1886, making him nine years the junior of Natsume Sōseki. Though both men shared an antipathy for the autobiographical writers of the Naturalist school that dominated Japanese letters in their day, they never traveled in the same literary or social circles. Unlike Sōseki, Tanizaki grew up in a strictly merchant-class family, thereby avoiding the inculcation of strict Confucian values in his childhood and the subsequent conflicts that would arise when those moral codes came into contact with modernization. The struggle of Tanizaki's youth was against unstable family finances, which threatened to cut short his educational career on several occasions.

Tanizaki's maternal grandfather, Kyūemon, was an interesting soul, a self-made man who started out as a clerk in a kettle shop and made a fortune through shrewd business sense and a little bit of luck. Kyūemon profited from the chaos that swept over Edo at the time of the Meiji Restoration in 1867: his boss at the kettle shop fled town, and Kyūemon simply took over the business. He went on from there to acquire an inn, a print shop, a lamp-lighting operation, a rice dealership, and a liquor store. Perhaps the most successful of Grandfather Kyūemon's many businesses was the Tanizaki Printing Company, which published a daily price list of rice. The Tokyo rice market was located near the family home at Kakigara-chō, and the immediate availability of price quotes made the little evening paper a hit.

A proud father who doted on his daughters, Kyūemon loathed to see them married off into the families of strangers, so he adopted young men into his own household to marry his daughters and manage his various businesses. One family, the Ezawas, provided two sons-in-law for Kyūemon. The Ezawas ran a sake wholesaler's in town, and Kyūemon got to know them well and lent them some money to keep their business running. When Mr. and Mrs. Ezawa both died in their thirties and an unscrupulous executor began manipulating the shop's finances, Kyūemon adopted two of the Ezawa boys. The elder was renamed Tanizaki Kyūbei, and he was married to Kyūemon's oldest daughter, Hana, and given charge of the rice store. The second Ezawa boy was renamed Tanizaki Kuragorō, and he was given the hand of Kyūemon's daughter Seki. It is this couple who gave birth to Tanizaki Jun'ichirō in the summer of 1886. The infant was listed in the family registry as the eldest son, though a male child born to the couple the previous year had died in his third day of life.

Tanizaki's mother, Seki, was so stunningly beautiful that she was asked to model for a poster that was widely displayed in the downtown *shitamachi* district of Tokyo. She retained her youthful looks so well that when she strolled around the town with her son Jun'ichirō, she was often mistaken for his sister.[8] Tanizaki idolized her, and as the years passed his fertile imagination created a compelling, idealized image that became the center of a lifelong obsession. He grafted images and impressions from other sources onto this key maternal figure—the Virgin Mary, the beauties from ukiyo-e prints, female-impersonator actors from the Kabuki stage, his own nursemaid—but his affection for the woman herself and a nostalgic yearning for the simple securities of childhood throbbed within him throughout his life.

Kuragorō was an unfortunate man, uniquely unsuited for a life in the business world. He suffered almost constant pain from a chronic stomach ailment, and Tanizaki would later speculate that his father's physical maladies perhaps contributed to his pathetic business performance. Grandfather Kyūemon did everything he could to provide Kuragorō with opportunities to succeed, and in each instance he failed miserably. Shortly after Jun'ichirō was born, Grandfather turned over management of the liquor store to Kuragorō, hoping that the young new family could support themselves off that portion of his holdings. In less than a year, Kuragorō managed to put the shop out of business (though it is difficult to envision a sudden drop in the demand for liquor), and the three were forced to move back in with Grandfather, sharing one room at the rear of the printing shop.

Next the lamp-lighting business was entrusted to Kura-gorō. It was a small operation, with a handful of employees who made the rounds of the neighborhood every evening to light the oil lamps that were still one of the main sources of illumination in the city. Shortly after Kuragorō got his hands on that business, however, Grandfather Kyūemon died of stomach cancer, and control of his businesses (and even his name) passed to his eldest son.

The scene surrounding Grandfather's deathbed is one that should have found its way into literature. Late in his life, Kyūemon had converted to the Greek Orthodox Church without telling his wife. The secret spilled out as he lay dying in the hospital, however, when a priest from the Nikolai Orthodox Church in Tokyo and a monk from the Nichiren Buddhist temple to which the family professed adherence crossed paths at the scene. A theological debate ricocheted over the dying man regarding the site of the "deceased's" funeral service and interment. Tradition triumphed, and after his death Kyūemon was laid to rest in the Nichiren cemetery as a devotee of that sect.

Jun'ichirō was only two when his grandfather died. He had no personal memories of him. But Kyūemon's influence upon his grandson extended beyond the grave. Tanizaki felt that his almost religious devotion to women was inherited from his grandfather, a reputed libertine in his youth, but most directly from his Grandfather's worship of the Virgin Mary.[9] In his memoirs of his childhood days, Tanizaki wrote:

> An icon of the Virgin Mary stood on a low cupboard.... When I looked at the image of the Virgin holding the infant Christ, there was a solemnness different from my emotions when I stood before the family Buddhist altar, as Grandmother and the others recited the sutras morning and evening. Gaz-

ing with inexpressible reverence into the Virgin Mother's eyes, so full of tenderness and mercy, I felt I never wanted to leave her side. I understood something of my grandfather's feelings as he prayed before this image of the Western goddess. There was a certain strangeness about it all, yet I sensed that someday I too might well do as he had done.[10]

Of course, Tanizaki never embraced religious faith as his grandfather had done, but he did elevate his adoration of women—particularly maternal women—to a level of zealousness equal to spiritual piety.

Not long after Grandfather's death, Kuragorō had a severe ulcer attack, perhaps brought on by the fact that he had managed to extinguish the lamp-lighting business for good. For a while he had to quit working altogether and recuperate at a hot springs. It was around this time that young Tanizaki, as if in an unconscious attempt to lose himself in pastimes and escape the increasingly depressing atmosphere at home, began to involve himself in an array of recreational activities. Initially, of course, the boy could have had no inkling that his forays into the world of *asobi*—of play, of games and amusements— would gradually become his means of reshaping what was a less-than-amusing reality at home, then at school, then in the world at large. Eventually, a preoccupation with constantly changing modes of *asobi* would become the driving force behind Tanizaki's friendships, his love affairs, and his fiction as well—precisely, in the latter case, when *asobi*'s antonym, *makoto*, a confessional sort of "seriousness," became the dominant tone in the writings of other Japanese authors.

When Tanizaki was only four, he had perhaps his first introduction to the potentialities of *asobi* and his initiation into the ways in which imagination might rework the details of daily life to his advantage. That year he began accompanying his mother and grandmother to Kabuki performances. Even though his family's finances were tight, these excursions were a luxury the women of the household were loath to relinquish. For the next eight years Tanizaki went at least once a year, and often twice, to see some of the most famous plays in the Kabuki repertoire performed by the most charismatic actors of the day. The vibrant mixture of color, music, dance, eroticism, and violence had a profound impact on the boy, and the contrast between the dismal circumstances at home and the larger-than-life rhythms and movements on the stage must have stimulated his imagination and sharpened his taste for a world of fantasy, a world where the dreariness of everyday life was crowded out by the splendors of a theatrical life taken to an extreme. After seeing the great actor Danjūrō perform, Tanizaki took advantage of every opportunity to mimic the performer's declamatory speech and elaborate posturings.[11] More than once this fantasy world would project itself onto the real circumstances of Tanizaki's life. One night, after seeing a famous historical play about the medieval warrior Benkei, Tanizaki came close to burning down the family house: decked out in Benkei's regalia, he had collided with an oil lamp suspended from the ceiling.

Sometimes his fantasies would crisscross the border between dream and reality:

> On nights when I had watched scenes of a woman about the same age as my mother having to part with a beloved child, or stabbed by a furious husband, or driven to kill herself for the sake of fidelity or chastity, I asked myself what Mother would do if she found herself in such straits.... Would she too abandon me or let me be killed for some principle? Thinking such thoughts, I passed along the streets that led toward home, swaying with the motion of the rickshaw.[12]

The transition from the realm of the stage back into the real world, where at home he would have to look on the glum face of his ineffectual father, was evidently a difficult one for the young Tanizaki.

Still, Jun'ichirō had come along before the family fortunes went into major decline, and as the oldest child he was almost shamelessly pampered.[13] And his parents undoubtedly tried to shield him from the effects of economic hardship. In 1890, after Kuragorō felt well enough to return to work and was given charge of a rice brokerage house, a second son was born. Seiji, as the child was named, would eventually become a writer and a professor of English literature at Waseda University. Writing in later days about his youth, he remarked that "both father and mother were good people, and loved their children well. We were poor, but I was comparatively happy at home."[14]

There is abundant evidence that Tanizaki's parents coddled and indulged him in his game playing. Despite their increasingly difficult economic position, they provided the boy with a nursemaid, Miyo, in whose arms he fell asleep each night. She was his constant companion throughout his childhood, at his side whenever he left the house. She was such a steady presence in his life that, looking back many years later, he could not be certain whether his earliest memories of a maternal figure represented his mother or Miyo.[15] This confusion of "mothers" is a significant feature of Tanizaki's writing, and forms the core of his late story, "*Yume no ukihashi*" (The Bridge of Dreams, 1959; trans. 1963). Some readers, in fact, have been startled or even repulsed by the story's main character, who continues to nurse into his teens, but there is a correlation, though not as extreme, in Tanizaki's own experience, a more mildly erotic form of *asobi* from his early years:

> Granny [as Tanizaki always called Miyo] used to say in later years that I suckled at my mother's breasts until I was six or so; and my memories bear this out: we were still living in the first house in Minami Kayaba-cho, and Seiji had already been born. After Mother had finished giving the breast to Seiji, I would sit on her lap, press at her breasts, and have my turn. "My, my—look at that! And him so big!" Granny would laugh as she watched us; and Mother would look a bit embarrassed as she continued to let me drink. It was not so much the taste of the milk that I craved as its sweet smell and the gentle warmth of Mother's breast.[16]

Mother seems to have been the one reliable anchor in Tani-zaki's young life, and one to which he would return, at least in his imagination, for solace when his own adult life became chaotic.

In 1892, after a year in kindergarten, Tanizaki entered the Sakamoto Primary School.[17] The regular school year began in April, but Tanizaki enrolled in September. The reason for the delay is simple: he stubbornly refused to start school at the usual time, and his parents let him get away with it. He was, he admitted, the lord of the roost at home and had his way with his parents. His fertile imagination, fanned by his visits to the Kabuki theater and indulged by his mother and nurse-maid, became a means of refashioning the frightening outside world. But once he stepped beyond their threshold, he was just another child. The security he felt in the bosom (as it were) of his family contrasted sharply with the anxiety he felt away from home. And so, of course, his nurse Miyo was en-listed to act as a buffer, accompanying him wherever he went. Even during his year in kindergarten, Miyo had to go with him into the classroom and sit directly beside him throughout the day. Without her there, he dissolved into tears.

The officials at the primary school were not as indulgent, feeling perhaps that it was time to develop a little indepen-dence. But even after Tanizaki had been persuaded to begin school a term behind the other children, he continued to act in a infantile manner.

> I insisted that Granny should always stay beside me as she had in kindergarten; but since the teacher could not allow nursemaids actually inside the classroom, poor Granny was forced to station herself in the hallway outside, so her face would always be visible to me through the corridor win-dow.... I soon became notorious throughout the school, for even among the first-graders there was no other crybaby quite on my scale.[18]

Whether it was because he was immature or because he

was insufferable, or whether it was that the pragmatic approach to learning at the school conflicted with his yearnings for *asobi*, Tanizaki managed to fail his first year and was forced to repeat with a new homeroom teacher. This second chance proved to be to his benefit, for the new teacher was capable and effective. Tanizaki may have hit it off immediately with Mr. Nogawa: they shared a common interest in the world of the theater (Mr. Nogawa frequently described the plots of his favorite plays to the class with dramatic enthusiasm) and in colored woodblock prints displaying beautiful women of the Edo period[19] as well (Tanizaki often sketched drawings of warriors and beautiful young women on his school slate[20]). Once he had earned the admiration and trust of Tanizaki, Mr. Nogawa was able to help him overcome his dread of studying, and indeed inspired him so effectively that by the end of the school year Tanizaki had the best marks of any student in the first-grade class. "Thanks to Mr. Nogawa," Tanizaki later wrote, "I came to realize that I was more talented than the average student, and so was freed from a sense of inferiority."[21]

Tanizaki made many close friends in primary school, but the one lifelong friendship he formed was with Sasanuma Gennosuke. Sasanuma was the only son of the owner of the Kairakuen, the first and, at that time, only Chinese restaurant in Tokyo. The wealthy Sasanuma family loved Tanizaki like one of their own, and Gennosuke taught him many "interesting" games and saw that he enjoyed many a hearty lunch.

The games Tanizaki learned to play with Sasanuma and his other friends did not, likely, go beyond the bounds of normal youthful curiosity, but they may also have sparked Tanizaki's imagination and provided him with materials for some of the stories of demonic childhood pastimes that he produced early in his writing career. When they were in second grade, Sasanuma (who was called Gen-chan) revealed to Tanizaki the secret of how babies were made, and this knowledge inspired them to create and enact in a storeroom of the restaurant a diverting little amusement which they called the "Emergency Basket" game: "A group of us, urged on by Gen-chan, started to make use of this space for a variety of games and pastimes. We would line up a number of the tables to make a stage and then perform a play on it. Or we would have pitched battles and hurl fire crackers at one another. Then one day someone had a fresh idea: we would 'play brothel'!..." Using baskets the size of large chests, they "converted them into 'courtesans' bedchambers' for our brothel game. Three or four of us would take turns, one playing the client, another the courtesan. Gen-chan and I each played both parts several times. We would lie facing each other in the narrow basket for a while—that was all; then another couple would take our place. Those who were not having their turn in the basket watched, snickering, from below."[22] As a result of such activities, Tanizaki and Sasanuma gained a reputation at school as "confirmed lechers."

By virtue of the family business, Sasanuma was also able to bring considerably more appetizing lunches (as far as Tanizaki was concerned) than any of the other boys. Sasanuma himself had grown weary of the rich leftovers from the Chinese restaurant, but students like Tanizaki were more than happy to exchange their paltry salted salmon for pork dumplings and a variety of other delicacies.

Although Tanizaki was beginning to succeed, both socially and academically, at school, his father continued to perpetuate his round of failures, this time as a rice broker. A third son was born to the family as the business continued its downward slide. Tanizaki's parents were faced with a painful decision: should they keep the new child, thus rendering life more difficult for every member of the family, or suffer the trauma of giving the child away? The choice was made right after the birth: the infant was sent to be raised by a foster family in Chiba prefecture. Tanizaki in later years expressed great sympathy for the anguish this must have cost his mother. She would endure the same agony twice more during her childbearing years.

With the financial burden of an additional child lifted, the family was able to continue enjoying a few simple pleasures: shell-gathering in the springtime, watching fireworks in the summer, and the occasional outings to the Kabuki theater, often sponsored by one of their uncles, who still occasionally picked up the tab for some of the Tanizaki family's amusements. But the strain of financial pressures on Seki was especially taxing, since she had been raised in privileged circumstances and spared the worries of household chores. As conditions worsened, however, she was forced to take on more such duties.

As Tanizaki's educational stock continued to rise in the classroom, culminating in his graduation at the top of his first-grade class in the spring of 1894, his father Kuragorō met with a disaster in the stock market, forcing him to close up his brokerage shop and move to a second house in Minami Kaya-ba-chō. This proved to be the most stable period of Tanizaki's youth: they remained in this house for a full eight years, and most of his clearest early memories occur here. For a time, Kuragorō worked with a stock trading firm in the Tokyo financial district, but this did little to change the family's situation, and Kuragorō grew increasingly depressed. Shortly after their move into the new house, a group of hired thugs came storming in, very likely to demand the payment of some outstanding debts. But Kuragorō sat frozen in misery and depression, and his appearance was so pathetic that the interlopers soon left of their own accord. Tanizaki recollects: "I became used to seeing that same tearful expression on Father's face over the succeeding years whenever some crisis occurred."[23]

The new house, selected as part of a belt-tightening program, was apparently on the gloomy side; at a time when many families in Tokyo were having electricity installed, the Tanizakis continued to use oil lamps—less out of fondness for Kuragorō's former venture in the lamp-lighting business than out of necessity—which rendered the house a dark and forlorn place. It was the kind of dwelling that Tanizaki in later years would aestheticize as typical of traditional Japanese culture: it was like a Kyoto teahouse, he said, highly impractical as a place to live, but attractive because it called up memories of former days. The ability to spread a patina of nostalgia over many diverse, childhood images, particularly at those times when his faddish infatuations turned sour, was one of Tanizaki's major achievements as a literary artist. His imagination flourished among shadows. His reminiscences of that time record his fears of ghosts, of badgers that transformed themselves into enormous monsters, of cunning foxes. Some of his phobias were derived from tales his mother and grandmother had told him, some from the Kabuki stage; others were founded upon actual experience. Once, when his Mother went into the outhouse late at night, she discovered a man trying to crawl up inside from the foul pit below. Her screams scared the intruder away, but the incident remained vivid in Tanizaki's mind, and was transformed into a literary scene of erotic worship in later years.

In the summer of 1894, the war between Japan and China broke out. Tanizaki displayed an early sign of literary talent by composing a poem in Chinese describing one of the Japan's initial victories. That same year, the profligate behavior of Tanizaki's uncle Kyūemon, who had taken over the family print shop, got the business into hot water, and it had to be sold off.

Around this time Tanizaki began to expand his range of cultural experience by taking in new forms of "play." In addition to the annual visits to Kabuki, which continued for another couple of years, he began to make the rounds of neighborhood shrines where local performers would put on dances and dramatic pieces based on historical legends. The performances were held on the same night every month, and Tanizaki went faithfully to each performance for a period of some six years. Many of these performances undoubtedly helped develop his budding aesthetic tastes. Although the plays, known as *chaban kyōgen*, began as comic farces, they soon began to respond to audience preferences and presented more and more scenes of swordfighting and bloody murders. In this sense, they were a kind of poor-man's Kabuki, and their concerns with historical setting and scenes of the grotesque surely influenced Tanizaki.

As a young man living behind the print shop, he had occasionally picked up copies of the literary magazine *Bungei Kurabu* (Literary Club) which were lying around in the parlor, his first exposure to the world of fiction, where his imagination would soon be released from the strictures of mundane experience. As a youth of ten, he became an avid reader of the new magazine for young people, *Shōnen Sekai* (Boys' World), which featured adventure stories and retellings of some of the classic Edo-period tales of heroic exploits. The tale that had the most impact on Tanizaki was a rewrite of Takizawa Bakin's heroic epic *Hakkenden* (Biographies of Eight Dogs, 1814–41); his next favorite work was a translation of Twain's *The Prince and the Pauper*. These books kindled his creative spirit as he passed through adolescence, and it is interesting to note that what moved him the most was the writers' ability to create a world of the imagination, a liberated kingdom where, once he had entered its portals, Tanizaki's mind was free to roam. He began, as he wrote, "to know the joys of letting the mind wander at will in an imaginary world, and to acquire the habit of yielding to those joys."[24] The important phrase here is the "yielding to those joys," the kind of surrender to the senses and to the power of the human imagination that is so crucial to an appreciation of Tanizaki's own writing.

In 1896 Seki gave birth to a daughter. There was discussion about sending her out to a foster family as they had with their previous son, but it was decided, since she was their first daughter, to keep her at home. Subsequent daughters were not so fortunate; and, in fact, this child would die at the age of fifteen from a tuberculin infection of the intestines.

That year, his last at primary school, Tanizaki began to

write. He had the encouragement of his teacher, but the great-est impetus came from a boy several years his senior named Nomura, who started producing a monthly literary journal called *Gakusei Kurabu* (Students' Club). It was, of course, limited in scope: each issue was handwritten in brush and ink; some seventy pages of manuscript were bound together and passed around among members of the club. Nomura was in full charge, creating the cover and illustrations himself, and assigning the other boys to write in the fields of biography, fiction, science, painting, calligraphy, and a column of miscel-lany. A makeshift "editorial office" was established at the Sasanumas' Chinese restaurant, where the club members would gather nearly every day to discuss each other's contri-butions.

After graduating from primary school, Tanizaki moved into the intermediate program, where his homeroom teacher was a Mr. Inaba. This gentleman, as inspired a teacher as Mr. Nogawa had been, was Tanizaki's original homeroom teacher the year he failed the first grade, and must have been delighted to see the academic progress the boy had made. Mr. Inaba re-mained Tanizaki's teacher for the four years of intermediate school, and with his vast knowledge of the Chinese and Japanese classics and an intense interest in Buddhist philoso-phy, he inspired Tanizaki in many ways. He was an eclectic instructor who combined the concepts of Edo-period neo-Confucianism with Zen thought, adding a dash of Western fla-vor from Plato and Schopenhauer. It is to Inaba's credit that he was able to arouse the interest of eleven-year-old boys in this type of subject matter, and Tanizaki describes his teach-ing techniques as innovative, liberated from the dryness of textbooks, and eclectic enough to draw lessons from whatever materials and opportunities presented themselves.

Mr. Inaba introduced his students to such Japanese clas-sics as Ueda Akinari's *Ugetsu monogatari* (Tales of Moon-light and Rain, 1776). Tanizaki recalls that he would copy out old texts by hand and make them available to the students.

Tanizaki read the "*Shiramine*" (White Peak) chapter from Akinari's tale collection so many times that he could recite the opening passage from memory. Inaba taught them from the Buddhist treatises of Kōbō Daishi, the great ninth-century sage; led them through the medieval poetry of Saigyō and Fujiwara Teika; opened their eyes to the world of the West by retelling episodes from the contemporary Japanese novel *Keikoku bidan* (Inspiring Instances of Statesmanship, 1883–84), which was set in ancient Greece; and inspired them with excerpts from Carlyle on British heroes.

Such an enlightened approach most certainly inflamed the curiosity of Mr. Inaba's students, but by his own admission Tanizaki in the end had only fleeting interest in much of what his teacher had to offer. It was one of the first of his many infatuations: "[Mr. Inaba's] real commitment was to the path of the ancient sages, and he seemed to want to educate me after a Confucian or Buddhist pattern. In the end, he was to be disappointed, for as I came to realize that my interest in philosophy, ethics, and religion was a temporary affectation, a mere borrowing from Mr. Inaba, and that my own province was to be that of pure literature, I found myself drifting away from him."[25]

Despite these later protestations, however, Tanizaki was clearly interested in acquiring knowledge on a variety of subjects at this age. Besides his regular studies, he enrolled in the Akika Academy, a center for the study of classical Chinese texts, and attended classes there for thirty minutes every morning before going to school. There he was trained in Confucius, Mencius, and works of history. In the afternoon, he attended the "Grand Academy of European Culture" run by four British women named Summers. This family, consisting of a mother and her three daughters, made up the entire teaching staff. One of the younger women, Lily (surely a coincidence that Tanizaki gave this name to the sly cat in his 1936 novel, *A Cat, a Man, and Two Women*), spoke fluent Japanese.

The atmosphere at the academy was unlike anything Tanizaki or his friends had ever experienced. They were over-whelmed by the beauty, dignity, and fundamental "strange-ness" of these foreign women, and felt, as did many Japanese of the time, that their fair complexions marked them off as su-perior beings. The Summers school was by all accounts the most stylish school of English operating in Tokyo in the late nineteenth century. Classes on the main floor, which constitut-ed the "normal curriculum," cost one yen per month, but the ladies also offered "special" classes on the second floor at the exorbitant monthly rate of fifteen yen. None of Tanizaki's cir-cle could afford the special course, and in fact the "normal" students were not allowed upstairs or even to pass through the sturdy door that led to the staircase. This climate naturally set the imaginations of the young boys spinning, filling their minds with fantasies, but also kept them attending the acade-my, though they realized that the teaching was slipshod and that they were learning little English.

Their imaginations were further pricked by the fact that their monthly receipts for tuition were scented with an exotic foreign perfume. Before long, the boys had clustered in Sasa-numa's room (where they often gathered to discuss sex) and were creating seductive rumors about these mysterious for-eign women: one boy had been told by his brothers that the Summers women (if, in fact, they actually were related to one another) entertained wealthy Japanese men on the second floor, and that the "special curriculum" involved something far more exciting than the study of English. There were fur-ther rumors that some of the most popular Kabuki actors of the day came to buy the favors of these women; another ver-sion maintained that it was the women who paid to enjoy the matinee idols. The rumors took on the shape of truth when the boys realized that all the "special" lessons were taught at night at the top of the forbidden staircase. The inquisitive boys hatched a plan to sneak up to the upper chamber one night and learn the truth.

Tanizaki never tells us whether the plan was actually carried out; it seems more likely from his own predisposition that he would have preferred to keep the fantasy intact and not test it against the facts. In any case, whether or not Madame Summers was operating an inventive cathouse from her language studio, it seems likely that the darkened upstairs rooms—filled with erotic secrets tinged with a sense of danger—that appear in some of Tanizaki's early stories can be traced back to his experiences at the "Grand Academy of European Culture."

Tanizaki published several pieces in *Students' Club* magazine, using such pen names as "Wanderer of the Moon and Flowers" and "Master of the Laughing Valley." A work of fiction he entered in a contest for the third issue won second prize. A story he published in the April 1898 issue featured a young student hero named Taniguchi Jun'ichirō, who, along with three of his friends, sets out to inspect firsthand the battlefields of the Sino-Japanese War. In the meanwhile, Tanizaki continued to read voraciously, saving up his allowance to buy books. His interests continued to be directed toward historical tales of adventure and some of the classics of the Japanese military era. To improve his own writing style, he would pluck out the most famous sections of classical texts and attempt to incorporate them in some way into his own writing. This interweaving of styles would become very important to him by the middle of his career, when he began interspersing original and fabricated historical documents in his fiction. He also memorized, with Mr. Inaba's encouragement, long passages from classics like the *Taiheiki* and *Heike monogatari*, and was said by his classmates to be able to stand and recite for thirty minutes at a time. Such a familiarity with the Japanese classics would also serve Tanizaki in good stead after he became a writer himself.

A second sister was born into the family in 1899; like the third son, she was sent to live with a foster family, this time a younger brother of Seki's. Another sister born in 1902 was shipped off to the same uncle's farm. Tanizaki finished intermediate school in 1901, and came very close to having this be the end of his education altogether, as well as the likely end to his literary aspirations. Tanizaki's father was willing to be patient while his eldest son completed his elementary education, but the burden of having a young, healthy boy in the house who required educational fees and contributed nothing to the meager family income became increasingly unbearable, and Kuragorō insisted that Tanizaki go to work after graduation.[26] When Tanizaki begged his father to let him continue with his studies, Mr. Inaba threw his support behind the request, urging Tanizaki's father to allow him at least to take the entrance exams. After Tanizaki passed with remarkable scores, and with the promise of financial assistance from Uncle Kyūbei and from the Sasanuma family of the Kairakuen restaurant, Kuragorō finally acquiesced, and in April Tanizaki entered the First Middle School at Hibiya.

That Kuragorō was not fully persuaded is evident from his attitude after Tanizaki completed his first year. With finances tighter than they had ever been, Kuragorō mustered what paternal authority he had and declared that his son's academic career must end. Once again forces of opposition had to be rallied in Tanizaki's defense. The list was impressive: in addition to Tanizaki himself, his supporters included the principal of his school, his Chinese literature teacher, and even, somehow, a member of the upper house of the Japanese Diet. But it took more than just moral support this time; there had to be some economic relief for the family. Although Tanizaki himself was not aware of it at the time, the Sasanuma family decided to invite their son's friend to move in with them. The Sasanumas asked Gennosuke to convey this offer to his classmate. Realizing that Tanizaki would end up working for the family like the several houseboys they already employed, Gennosuke feared for his comrade's self-esteem and never told him about the option.[27] This would not, however, be the last time that the Sasanumas would display noble generosity toward Tanizaki.

Fortunately the teacher of Chinese did some hasty footwork and arranged for Tanizaki to work as a live-in tutor and houseboy for the Kitamura family, who operated the Seiyōken restaurant at Tsukiji (those who marvel at the nearly obsessive interest in food displayed in Tanizaki's fiction and essays would do well to recall how much of his youth was spent in restaurants!). Tanizaki remained with the Kitamuras for five years, living with two of the family's sons on the second floor of a food store they ran separately from the restaurant. The experience was not always pleasant for him. Mrs. Kitamura, eager to test the honesty of the young man they had taken in, sent him one day to the bank with one more banknote than she had recorded on the deposit slip.[28] Tanizaki passed this test with flying colors.

At school, Tanizaki was performing exceptionally well: after the first semester of his second year, he took a by-pass examination and skipped into the second semester of the third year. In addition, his writing was flourishing. At the age of seventeen, Tanizaki was publishing essays and Chinese poetry with regularity in the literary journal of the middle school. He wrote on a wide array of topics, treating the medieval Buddhist activist Nichiren; the poetry of Saigyō; a critique of "oriental" pessimism, in which he argued that the philosophies of Asia were too dark in their denial of the joy that must be a part of human existence; and a work titled "Moral Concepts and Aesthetic Concepts," in which he cited Carlyle, Dante, and Shakespeare to bolster his arguments. In September of 1903, he became the head of the school association which published the literary journal, indicating the respect in which he was held by his peers. One of them, Tatsuno Yutaka, has written:

> Around the time we entered our fourth year, those of us who were lazy in every respect finally came to the realization that Tanizaki was a fellow blessed with unusual talents. We concluded that when it came to literature, you could ask Tanizaki anything and he could tell you about it.... During composition class, when we were given a topic to write about,

we'd secretly have Tanizaki whisper some ideas to us, and if we took his suggestions and expanded haphazardly upon them, papers that we'd always gotten C's on sometimes turned into B papers.

One day during composition, we were given the topic, "the beauty of nature." While we sat with our heads in our hands, not having any idea what we should write, Tanizaki whipped off two poems and turned them in. One of them was later published in a magazine.[29]

Tanizaki was evidently not as skilled in athletic events as he was at writing. Tatsuno remembers:

Whenever he hung from the chinning bar, he would just remain there dangling, so there was no hope for him to make it over the vaulting horse. He came charging desperately toward the vault. Watching from the sidelines, we all thought, "Be careful!" Tanizaki had no idea he was supposed to slow down as he approached the vault, and when he planted both hands on the horse's flank, the thrust of his body continued to propel him forward, smashing the bridge of his nose into the side of the horse. He collapsed to the side and his face was buried in the sand. When he finally staggered to his feet, his face was covered with sand, and blood gushing from his nose had painted his chin red.[30]

Graduation from middle school came in March of 1905, and with the continued financial assistance of the Kitamuras, Tanizaki was able to advance without interruption into the department of English Law at the First Higher School. He was nineteen years old. There can be little question that the choice of major was made under pressure from the Kitamura family, who did not want him studying literature. But it also appears that, at this time at least, Tanizaki took into consideration the practical possibility that he might need a career like law to support himself while he worked on his writing as a side venture. He did, though, join the literary society at school, and in 1907 he took over as editor of their magazine.

In June of that year, the Kitamuras intercepted a love letter which Tanizaki had written to another of their live-in employ-ees, an eighteen- or nineteen-year-old maid named Fukuko who had come to their home two years earlier to learn eti-quette. She apparently learned quite a bit more, thanks to Tanizaki, and when the family discovered the affair, the young lovers were expelled from the house. Fukuko went back to live with her family in Hakone, but Tanizaki contin-ued to visit her there for some time after their ouster. Within five years she had died of pneumonia. The experience provid-ed Tanizaki with materials for the stories he published in the high school literary magazine, and for a novel he began in 1912 but never completed.

No longer under the constraints imposed on him by the Kitamuras, and having tasted the joys of sensual indulgence, Tanizaki strengthened his determination to become a writer, and switched his major from English law to English literature. He moved into a dormitory, where he began to live his newly discovered life of decadence to the full. This was a time, his friend Hamamoto Hiroshi has written, when decadence was the "in" thing for young people, just as fashionable Marxism was the accepted mode for young intellectuals just after World War II. It was the kind of behavior that was perfectly natural for (in fact, expected of) anyone who aspired to a ca-reer in literature. Evidently Tanizaki and virtually all of his as-sociates in the literary society contracted some form of vene-real disease.[31]

Although Tanizaki was popular and highly admired by his literary colleagues at school, his attitudes and behavior did not win the favor of his fellow dormitory residents. Many of the young men who were living in the dorm at the First Higher School had come from the provinces, and felt a mixture of in-feriority and animosity toward the brash and often patronizing "Edokko" natives of Tokyo, that wondrous breed immortal-ized by the title character in Sōseki's *Botchan*. Tanizaki seems to have gone out of his way to alienate these country types, boasting unsparingly about his proud Edo origins and denigrating all unfortunate country bumpkins. His haughtiness at this stage seems to have been based almost exclusively on pride of place; later he would transform this attitude into a literary stance, placing himself above the writers who belonged to the autobiographical Naturalist school, most of whom had come to Tokyo from outlying regions.

The liberation which Tanizaki found in his personal life seems to have taken the wind out of his desire to succeed in his studies. He became a typically lazy student, propping copies of Chikamatsu's plays behind his textbooks in class; playing the role of the elegant Edo townsman by indulging in morning baths topped by a tofu breakfast; and displaying more interest in the latest news from the Kabuki theater than the subject matter taught by his teachers.[32] After graduating from high school in July of 1908 at the age of twenty-two, he entered the Japanese literature department at Tokyo Imperial University—not because he had developed an interest in the academic approach to literature, but because he was certain that it would be one of the easiest programs at the school, one which would leave him enough free time to write his own fiction.[33]

His parents, meanwhile, had just abandoned a six-year attempt to run a boarding house and moved back to their original neighborhood in Nihonbashi. About the same time, a final child was born to the family, this time a son. Out of work and out of money, Tanizaki himself had to move back in with them while he started college. It was an unfortunate situation: while he had been living alone, his interests had diverged significantly from those of his parents; he had passed his sexual initiatory rites; he was by turns annoyed with and grieved by his younger sister, who was fading away with tuberculosis; and he often argued with his parents, who now saw him primarily as an incorrigible leech. He tried to avoid his home as much as possible, instead flitting between the Kairakuen restaurant, a summer house owned by the Sasanumas, and the dorm rooms of tolerant friends. The family had to pawn many

of their belongings just to eke out a living, and discord over finances made his mother habitually hysterical.[34] The situation
became so unbearable that Tanizaki developed a case of nervous exhaustion, which would occasionally manifest itself in
bizarre paroxysms of fear, the most common of which was
fear of boarding a train or any other moving vehicle. He retained a fear of earthquakes instilled by his mother. Her dread
of thunder he had overcome as a teenager.

His neurasthenia grew so severe that he left home early in
1909 to rest at another villa owned by the Sasanumas; there he
read the account of a sojourn in America written by Nagai
Kafū, an Edo-style dilettante writer who was soon to become
Tanizaki's literary mentor and kindred spirit. Tanizaki was so
impressed by Kafū's *Tales of America* that he vowed that
once he had established himself as a writer, the first person
whose admiration he hoped to gain was Kafū's. That wish
was to be granted. While at the villa, Tanizaki wrote a play
and a short story which he sent to two separate, established literary journals. The play was rejected, and the manuscript of
the story was lost. Discouraged, he briefly considered drop-
ping out of school and becoming a newspaper reporter in
northern Japan, though he soon abandoned the idea.

Back in Tokyo and in his own lodgings in early 1910,
Tanizaki fell in love with one of the attractive waitresses at
the Kairakuen. Determined to marry her, he presented his plan
to Sasanuma, who gave his consent. Tanizaki then dragged his
mother along to the restaurant to have a look at the prospective bride. She approved, and Tanizaki formally proposed
marriage through Sasanuma as intermediary. He received a
flat rejection.[35]

That September, Tanizaki participated in the publication
of a new literary journal, *Shinshichō* (New Currents of
Thought).[36] The chief moving force behind the magazine was
Osanai Kaoru, soon to become a major figure in the creation
of modern Japanese drama; the staff included Watsuji Tetsu-
rō, one of twentieth-century Japan's leading philosophers. It

was not that the university did not have a magazine already. Tanizaki and his comrades, however, having worked on school magazines since their elementary days, were accustomed to having complete artistic control over their work. When they entered Tokyo Imperial University, they found that the only magazine available to them was the rather musty *Teikoku Bungaku*, where they would have to join with graduates of other high schools and have some stranger decide what would be published. Since this did not suit their style, the malcontents got together and created their own journal. Thus *Shinshichō* came into being.[37]

The first obstacle these aspiring writers had to surmount was, of course, economic. None of them had the means to fund a journal that aimed for an initial publication of five hundred copies. Once again it was the Sasanuma family who came to Tanizaki's aid. His old school chum, Gennosuke, earnestly hoped to see his talented friend succeed as a writer, and though he had no interest in literature himself, he put up the money to produce the new journal.

In the first issue of *Shinshichō* Tanizaki published the play "*Tanjō*" (Birthday), which had earlier been rejected by a mainstream magazine. This period play was set in the Heian court and based on materials from historical tales and the diary of Murasaki Shikibu. Unfortunately, a piece that Osanai wrote for the premier issue created a second major problem for the magazine—censorship.[38] Tanizaki had to contend with unenlightened government censors throughout much of his career, culminating most notoriously in the banning of the first serialization of *The Makioka Sisters* in 1941. Although on this first occasion the fault was not Tanizaki's, it was later most often his work that raised the censor's hackles.

Although *Shinshichō* lasted only seven issues, the third contained his best-known early work, "*Shisei*" (The Tattooer; trans. 1963). Tanizaki's association with the magazine also put him in contact with a number of important literary figures. In November the first meeting of a group of anti-Naturalist writers, dubbed *Pan no kai* (The Devotees of Pan), was held at a Western-style restaurant in Nihonbashi. There Tanizaki met Nagai Kafū. A month later, when Kafū attended a rehearsal for a play being presented at Osanai Kaoru's Free Theater, Tanizaki presented him with a copy of the journal containing "The Tattooer."

In many respects "The Tattooer" is a prime attack on the Naturalist form of literature prevailing in Japan at the time. The famous opening of the story declares: "It was a time when people still possessed the noble virtue of 'playfulness' (*oroka*)." The word *oroka*, with its connotations of foolishness, silliness, and triviality, is the ideal antonym for the word most prized by the confessional writers of I-novels: *makoto*, or sincerity carried to an extreme. Certainly Tanizaki was aware of the gauntlet he was hurling in the faces of his literary foes. The great irony of the story, however, is that Tanizaki had originally composed the tale in a modern setting, but before it appeared in print, he realized that it called for an Edo-period atmosphere, and shifted it back to what was, in his imagination at least, a time of noble foolishness. The tattooer's single-minded dedication to his art, his quest for beauty that concludes when he glimpses a perfect female foot, and his groveling submission before the work of art he has carved into the flesh of a ravishing, domineering woman—these prominent and uncommon elements of the story appear in many other forms over the course of Tanizaki's career.

In the few months after "The Tattooer" was published, Tanizaki received requests for manuscripts from some of the leading journals of the day. The most important of the people to come knocking at his door was Takita Choin, editor of the prestigious magazine *Chūō Kōron*, who called on Tanizaki in November of 1911 and asked for a submission. Tanizaki had already received his first manuscript fee from another journal early that year, but the invitation to publish in *Chūō Kōron*, which would be his primary publisher for the rest of his life, was most welcome. Virtually everything but writing (family, college, a place to live) he now pushed to the back of his mind. "For me art came first and life second. At first I strove to make my life accord, insofar as possible, with my art, or else to subordinate it to my art,"[39] he wrote of this period. As if in unspoken submission to that rearrangement of his priorities, Tanizaki's grandmother and tuberculin sister both died that spring, and when notice came from the university that Tanizaki would not be allowed to graduate in July unless he made a tuition payment he had neglected because of his absorption in writing, he simply chucked school altogether and went on with his career. Nothing else mattered.

Then in November came the big break: in that month's issue of the journal *Mita Bungaku*, Nagai Kafū, who was, after all, a fellow decadent with his heart firmly planted in the mystique of the Edo period, published an essay lauding Tanizaki as a writer. The article is as famous as it was influential. Kafū later claimed that he wrote the essay as a favor to the publisher who was about to issue Tanizaki's first collection of stories. This publisher, fearful that the volume would be banned by the censors, pleaded with Kafū to use his influence to legitimize Tanizaki as a serious young writer. Whatever the motivation, readers at the time were impressed by Kafū's effusive praise: "Tanizaki Jun'ichirō has succeeded in exploiting the domain of art that nobody else in the Meiji literary world has hitherto been able to, or even desired to exploit. To put it in other terms: Tanizaki Jun'ichirō possesses to the full certain rare qualities that none of our many other writers today possesses."[40] Kafū proceeded to enumerate the "rare qualities" he discerned in Tanizaki's writing: 1) a quality of mystery and profound beauty (*shinpi yūgen*) that resulted from feelings of "carnal fear" (*nikutai-teki kyōfu*), an intense pleasure in response to physical cruelty. Such a quality could be applied as easily to Kabuki, and in fact Kafū likened this aspect of Tanizaki's work to Kabuki murder scenes which simultaneously evoked both agony and beauty; 2) a focus exclusively upon life in the city; and 3) an already perfected literary style.[41]

Thanks to Kafū's acclamation, Tanizaki, then twenty-five, was able to launch himself into the literary world,[42] and his first story collection, *The Tattooer*, was published in December of 1911. He remained a devout follower of Kafū, but he similarly did not forget to express his gratitude to others who had helped him. Shortly after the collection was published, he placed a copy in his pocket and paid a visit to a Buddhist temple in Asakusa, where the mother of Sasanuma Gennosuke of the Kairakuen had been buried half a year earlier. Beside her grave, he bowed his head to the ground, reported his accomplishments to her, and presented the book to her headstone.[43]

Tanizaki had achieved initial success as a writer, but he had left all other considerations by the wayside. No longer comfortable at home, he began a life of vagabond wandering, moving from one temporary lodging to another. This was, as one of his close friends noted, something of a fashion among young literary types of the day, a pilgrimage like those of medieval poet-monks, combining the literary and the spiritual. Tanizaki meandered from Tsugaru in the north to the Kinki district in the south, a satchel containing his manuscripts tucked under his arm.[44]

He soon began rubbing shoulders with some of the most important figures in Japan's artistic world. Takita, the editor at *Chūō Kōron*, who had taken a liking to him, invited Tanizaki to a New Year's party attended by many literary luminaries. He traveled leisurely around the Kyoto area, his pockets filled with money from newspaper advances, in the company of such well-known writers as Iwano Hōmei (perhaps the most "artistic" of the I-novelists) and Ueda Bin. This was a heady ascent from poverty and obscurity for a young man of twenty-six, but it did not prevent Tanizaki from boldly carving out his own unique literary niche. Some of the stories in his *Tattooer* collection dealt with transvestitism, a group of children who engage in sado-masochistic games, and other previously tabooed subjects.

Many works from the next couple of years seem to aim at

stretching the limits of acceptability to the breaking point, almost a kind of cat-and-mouse game with the censors, which Tanizaki more and more frequently lost. One can almost detect a masochistic desire in the stories Tanizaki wrote in the late teens of the twentieth century. His primary influences during this period, which is often referred to as his period of "diabolism" because of the story "*Akuma*" (The Devil, 1912–13), were not merely foreign, but decidedly off-beat foreign. The most commonly cited sources of inspiration are such dark masters as Edgar Allan Poe and Oscar Wilde, with the studies of pathology by Krafft-Ebing likewise a clear influence. However revolting specific passages in these works may be, and however much Tanizaki deserved his reputation as a panderer to exotic tastes, it is evident that he is groping to formulate a fundamental view of human behavior quite distinct from that of his contemporaries: a view which essentially insists that the "facts of history" can reveal only superficial trivia about any single human being, and that the "truth" about an individual is most often buried so deeply and so darkly within the chambers of the mind, where sexual urges blind the reason and dominate the will, that they can never fully be known to others. This focus upon the unknowability of human motivation is one which Tanizaki shares with many great writers of the modern era, Sōseki among them. The manner in which these mysteries are probed is profoundly different between the Apollonian intellectual Sōseki and the Dionysian hedonist Tanizaki, but the culminating view of mankind is surprisingly similar.

It is not surprising that Tanizaki would seek out such foreign models as Wilde, one of the least tame of nineteenth-century objectors to the common morality; Tanizaki even translated Wilde's play *Lady Windermere's Fan* into Japanese in 1919. Wilde's unofficial motto, that the life of art was superior to the art of life, was transformed into one of Tanizaki's own, and in a 1931 essay Tanizaki insisted: "The influence that Western literature has exerted on us has taken many forms, without any question. One of the most important, in my view, has been the 'emancipation of love,' or, to take it one step further, 'the emancipation of sexual desire.'"[45] In that sense, Tanizaki's infatuation with Western literature can be seen as part of a larger literary undertaking, the freeing of himself from conventional restraints which would allow him to probe those previously dark and tabooed avenues of human desire that he felt central to understanding why people behave as they do.

Infatuations with various women speckle this period as well: the proprietress at an inn at Kyōbashi; an unknown woman in Hakone[46] for whom Tanizaki composed the poem, "Crossing the mountain road to Hakone by night / I saw the steam rising from the hot bath / Where my love washes her raven hair,"[47] and over whom Tanizaki briefly flirted with the notion of love suicide. His romantic quest seems to have reached a conclusion in May of 1915, when he married Ishikawa Chiyo, who at nineteen was ten years his junior. The ceremony was carried out in conventional fashion, with Sasanuma Gennosuke and his wife acting as the official go-betweens. The newlyweds set up their own household, and soon were receiving guests and family. A frequent visitor was Chiyo's younger sister, Seiko, still a teenager, who would before long become an important player in Tanizaki's game of life. Ten months after the wedding a daughter, Ayuko, was born to the couple. Tanizaki was more than a bit ambivalent about becoming a father; like General Jack Ripper in *Dr. Strangelove*, he feared the experience would drain him of his precious creative fluids. When Ayuko was a month old, he admitted that he still had not been able to muster any affection for her, and perhaps never would. He concluded that if another child came along, he would put it up for adoption, as his parents had.[48] He never had to face that eventuality.

His infatuation with Chiyo, if such it can be called, chilled quickly, a fact that shows in his writing. His stories from this period, including "*Otsuya koroshi*" (The Murder of Otsuya,

1915; trans. as "A Springtime Case," 1926), are still very much under the sway of his fascination with the dark side of Edo culture and attempt to capture the feel of the Kabuki stage in print; they often center around a venomous woman. Many of these stories ran afoul of the censors, and from a mixture of frustration and spite Tanizaki began producing works that seem almost smug parodies of the self-exploratory I-novels of the Naturalists, who fared better with the authorities because of their purported sincerity and "scientific" exploration of the self. These are stories such as "*Shindō*" (Child Prodigy) and "*Oni no men*" (Demon Mask) of 1916, and the novella *Itansha no kanashimi* (The Sadness of a Rebel, 1917), which he described as his "only book of confessions."[49]

Tanizaki had become disaffected with Chiyo as early as 1916 (the year, incidentally, in which Sōseki died); some critics have suggested that she was not sufficiently sadistic when it came to bedroom games.[50] In any case, Tanizaki began treating her with open contempt and publicly lamented his marriage. By the following year, he had moved Chiyo and their daughter out of the house (they went to live with Tanizaki's parents[51]) and invited in his sister-in-law Seiko (who, evidently, was a better game player) in Chiyo's stead. Since it is generally agreed that Seiko was the model for the character Naomi in Tanizaki's 1924 novel *Chijin no ai* (A Fool's Love; trans. as *Naomi*, 1985), a Japanese flapper whose Western-style beauty and domineering ways delight the cowering male protagonist, it seems quite likely that Seiko was more amenable to Tanizaki's proclivities. Seiko had, according to contemporary accounts, a Western mien (Naomi is described as resembling a "Japanese Mary Pickford"), and soon manifested hopes of becoming a film star. She was, in short, a young woman inclined to flirt with things new, modern, and stimulating, making her more appealing than Chiyo (stable wife and mother), and more in keeping with the tastes of a man who wrote that he preferred the sort of women he saw in foreign films: "What I sought were lively eyes, a cheerful expression and a clear voice, a body that was healthy and well-proportioned, and above all, long straight legs and adorable feet with pointed toenails cased in snugly fitting high-heeled shoes—in short, a woman with the physique and clothes of a foreign star."[52]

In 1917 Tanizaki formed friendships with two kindred writers who were to remain important to him for many years. In January, the young short-story writer Akutagawa Ryūnosuke came calling to pay his respects, and they became fast friends. In the same year, Tanizaki made the acquaintance of Satō Haruo, a poet and story writer, whose eventual relationship with Tanizaki had less to do with literature than with romantic triangles. Increasingly Tanizaki's home became a gathering place for writers like Akutagawa, Satō, and others who felt disaffected with the confessional mainstream of contemporary literature and inclined to inventive, aesthetic approaches to writing.

In May of that year, Tanizaki was vacationing in the mountains of Gunma prefecture when word came that his mother, Seki, had had a heart attack and was near death. Before he left Tokyo, she had been stricken with a case of erysipelas, a streptococcal infection which tainted her legendarily beautiful face with red, crusty blisters, but because she had been on the mend, he had left for the mountains. By the time he rushed back to be at her bedside, she was already dead. He wrote:

> Without even changing out of my travel clothes I went up to the body, now cold, and lifted the small, thin towel covering her face. The last ugly traces of erysipelas had disappeared; and that beautiful face, which had once graced the local town posters and caused not a few to mistake her for my sister, was now as pure and clear as porcelain.[53]

Seki was only fifty-three. Beginning with his dreamlike pursuit of her image in "*Haha o kouru ki*" (Longing for Mother), which he began serializing in 1918, through his late story

"Bridge of Dreams," Tanizaki continued to idealize, and embellish on, his mental and emotional portrait of his mother.

In the fall of 1918, Tanizaki went to Korea, Manchuria, and the Chinese mainland, traveling about on his own for over a month. There was, apparently, no literary or intellectual purpose to the trip; it more closely resembled the "sex-tours" that some unenlightened Japanese men still take today. Not long after his return, his father suffered a brain hemorrhage, and Tanizaki moved in with his family at the rice shop. By February of the following year, Kuragorō was dead. Tanizaki turned the rice shop over to relatives and moved to a new home, where under one roof he assembled his wife and daughter, a younger sister and brother, and the sister-in-law with whom he was romantically involved. A move at the end of that year to Odawara marked Tanizaki's final break with Tokyo: never again would he live in that city.

His fascination with the new and the foreign, however, continued apace. He published translations of some of Beaudelaire's prose poems, and in 1920 he became a script consultant for the newly formed Taishō Motion Picture Studios in Yokohama. His official duties required his presence at the studio once a week, but he became so involved in the writing of screenplays and participating in the production process that he ended up being there over half of each month. The first scenario he produced for the studio was titled *Amachua kurabu* (Amateur Club), and though the story was a comedy about would-be actors attempting to stage a Kabuki play at the seaside, in both style and tone it was more reminiscent of contemporary Hollywood farces. The director, Thomas Kurihara, was a Japanese who had studied film making in California, where he had worked with Sessue Hayakawa and William S. Hart.[54] The star of *Amateur Club* was none other than Tanizaki's paramour, Seiko, who not only adopted the screen name Hayama Michiko, but appeared in the film's first scene in a bathing suit and began flirtatious relationships with many of the men on the set (her fickleness recalling the title character in *Naomi*).

The film proved unsuccessful: it was too American, audiences felt. A third screenplay, a 1921 adaptation of "*Jasei no in*" (The Lasciviousness of the Viper) in Ueda Akinari's *Ugetsu monogatari* (which Tanizaki had read under Mr. Inaba's tutelage in intermediate school), was far more popular. As a result of his fleeting interest in motion pictures, Tanizaki's attention was diverted from the writing of fiction: two major novels started around this time were abandoned incomplete. But he continued to write short stories, many of them thrillers dealing not merely with "evil" wives, but with men's schemes to have their wives eliminated. "*Tojō*" (On the Way, 1920), the best of them, details the methodical manner in which a detective gathers clues to prove that a woman's death, apparently from natural causes, was actually murder at the hands of her husband, who wished her out of the way so he could marry another woman. Some critics regard "On the Way" as the beginnings of the Japanese detective-story genre.

Toward the end of 1920, Tanizaki's good friend, the poet Satō Haruo, stopped by Odawara on his way back from China and Taiwan. Satō was appalled at the callous manner in which Tanizaki treated his wife, Chiyo, and before long had asked that he be allowed to marry her himself. The notion was appealing to Tanizaki, but at the last minute, when both Satō and Chiyo had their hopes pinned on this resolution, Tanizaki changed his mind. No satisfactory explanation for this shift in attitude has been offered, and to suggest that Tanizaki was simply involved in another of his sado-masochistic games is less than satisfactory. At any rate, the close friendship between the two men was destroyed by this affair, an event which the papers dubbed "the Odawara Incident."

For reasons which only he could explain (and never did), Tanizaki was more solicitous toward Chiyo in the aftermath of the incident, at least on the surface. (Did he, in fact, enjoy tormenting her with kindness, or hope that his attitude would elicit an exquisitely cruel response?) After completing his fourth scenario for Taishō Studios he turned in his resignation (realizing they were more interested in sentimental romantic tragedies than the kind of "art" film he wished to create), and in September of 1921 moved his family to the foreign district of Yokohama. There he led an increasingly "exotic" existence, dressing only in Western clothes, wearing shoes (rather than Japanese footwear) throughout the day, learning to play the guitar, resuming his studies of English conversation, and, all in all, living the kind of life he would describe for Jōji, the male protagonist in *Naomi*. In 1922 he wrote:

> My [wife's] younger sister [Seiko] learned to dance from a Western friend and got the rest of the family interested. Her first pupil was my daughter, who's seven this year.... I began to take lessons from a real teacher, a Russian named Vasily Krupin, who lives in Yokohama and gives lessons twice a week on the second floor of a certain cafe.... Dancing makes a person feel young, cheerful, and lively, which alone is enough to make it far better than a teahouse party. Besides, it's economical.[55]

He was trying, in every conceivable manner, to live a Westernized life. On January 30, 1923, notices appeared in newspapers that Tanizaki, then thirty-seven, would soon be leaving for the West. There is no telling what kind of person or writer he might have become had he realized his dream of living overseas as his idol Kafū had. But the dream, as we will see in a moment, was never realized. Several years later, looking back at this period of slavish imitation of what he presumed was the mode of Western life, Tanizaki would write of himself: "It is not my intention to debate here whether having been influenced by the West was beneficial or harmful to my writings, but no one knows as well as I—to my great embarrassment—in what extremely superficial, indeed mindless ways this influence revealed itself."[56]

In 1923 Tanizaki had no such perspective on his behavior, and it seems likely that he was indeed making serious preparations for a trip abroad. He spent most of the month of August

with his family at a hotel in Hakone. They returned to Yokohama on the twenty-seventh, and four days later Tanizaki left
for Hakone alone. The next day, while he was riding in a char-
coal-powered bus there, the Great Kanto Earthquake struck,
killing over 100,000 people in the Tokyo area. The tremors
were felt as far as Hakone, and Tanizaki's bus lurched danger-
ously, though no one was injured. The government immediately banned all train or highway travel into the cities of
Tokyo and Yokohama to prevent greater confusion or loss of
life, so on September 4 Tanizaki set out on a circuitous route
to rejoin his family in Yokohama. He rode the train to Osaka,
obtained a manuscript advance from a newspaper there,[57] and
on the ninth boarded the ship *Shanghai-Maru* at the port of
Kobe. The boat docked in Yokohama on the tenth, and on the
following day, eleven days after the quake, he found his family safe at the home of a writer friend in Tokyo. Nine days later
he took his wife and daughter and again boarded the *Shanghai-Maru*, which returned them to Kobe. They moved three
times before the end of the month in the Kansai area, finally
settling in a house in Kyoto.

As students of Tanizaki's life have frequently noted, this
move to western Japan was intended as a temporary refuge,
from which Tanizaki was expected to return to the Tokyo–
Yokohama area and resume his foreign ways. Though initially
he felt concern over the earthquake, his second reaction was,
"How marvelous! Tokyo will become a decent place now!"
He had a vision of the city that would be rebuilt from the destruction: "Orderly thoroughfares, shiny, newly paved streets,
a flood of cars, blocks of flats rising floor on floor, level on
level in geometric beauty, and threading through the city elevated lines, subways, streetcars. And the excitement at night
of a great city, a city with all the amusements of Paris or New
York, a city where the night life never ends. Then, and then
indeed, the citizens of Tokyo will come to adopt a purely Eu-
ropean-American style of life, and the young people, men and
women alike, will all wear Western clothes. This is the in-

evitable trend of the times, and whether one likes it or not, this is what will happen."[58] One hesitates to call Tanizaki prophetic, though his description of the city, minus the "geometric beauty" and the "night life," seems quite accurate from today's perspective. But for whatever combination of reasons—and one must speculate that his infatuations with Seiko, with motion pictures, with ill-fitting Western suits and shoes, were beginning to pall—Tanizaki remained in the Kyoto–Kobe area for the next twenty years. He would only leave when enemy bombing raids threatened to destroy the entire region, and with it the traditional culture he had grown to love.

The serialization of *Naomi*, which Tanizaki began in the Osaka edition of the *Asahi* newspaper in March of 1924, met with considerable opposition both from censors and from the more conservative reading public in western Japan. After only four months, the paper suspended publication of the work, and Tanizaki had to wait five more months before he could resume and ultimately conclude it in a magazine. His Kansai readers evidently were shocked by the depictions of the vulgar extremes to which the "modern girls" (*moga* was the abbreviated translation in Japanese) and "modern boys" (*mobo*) of decadent Tokyo would go in their attempts to live like Western dilettantes. What they missed, of course, was the subtle attitude of satire that Tanizaki gradually came to inject into the story, as he himself pulled slowly away from an enchantment with such a life. No reader today would imagine that Tanizaki's portrayal of an abjectly subservient Jōji and a giddily promiscuous Naomi were intended to be portraits of exemplary lives, any more than our current perspective would let us concur with the wartime view that Tanizaki was being critical of the carefree, cultured bourgeois life in the opening passages of *The Makioka Sisters*.[59] It must have given Tanizaki a delectable and ambivalent mixture of pleasure and pain when the young people in Tokyo began to model themselves after Jōji and Naomi, even coining the term "Naomi-ism" to describe the kind of modish Roaring Twenties life they thought they were leading.

The changes in Tanizaki's attitudes toward the West, and his gradual move toward more traditional tastes, began to manifest themselves in subtle ways. He spent a month in China in early 1926; this time, however, he was not on the continent to satisfy his incontinent passions. He contacted a number of Chinese intellectuals and writers, including Kuo Mo-jo and T'ien Han, and kept in touch with them in the years ahead.[60] Upon his return, he traveled extensively around western Japan, visiting such centers of traditional culture as Yoshino (famed for its cherry blossoms), Nara (the seat of traditionalist Yamato culture), and Awaji island (where the primitive puppet plays described in *Some Prefer Nettles* are performed). Likely enough his almost imperceptible shift toward the old Japan was not the result of a conscious decision to abandon the West and embrace the native past; most certainly this transformation started out as many of his other pursuits had, as an infatuation with a culture that was new and, therefore by definition, stimulating to him. He wrote, in fact, that "I loved the old Japan as a form of exoticism, in precisely the sense that a foreigner treasures the prints of Hiroshige."[61]

Like an addict of erotica, Tanizaki approached this new interest with a sensuous fervor. His responses to such enticing stimuli followed familiar patterns. Typical was his attempt in April of 1926 to acquire what he hoped would be a pornographic delight. That month, he wrote a friend in Shanghai giving careful instructions on how to slip an illustrated copy of the *Arabian Nights* past Japanese customs.[62] Kaname, the hero of *Some Prefer Nettles*, emulates this attempt, but is thoroughly disappointed when the volumes arrive and he finds them utterly lacking in erotic value. Had Tanizaki's initial fascination with traditional Japanese culture followed this standard pattern, he would have approached it with a combination of childlike delight and adolescent erotic yearning. But this time the pattern was broken.

One could speculate endlessly over why this particular infatuation, among so many, was transformed into an enduring love, and why he did not eventually abandon his interest in classical Japan and the culture of the Kansai as he had his previous obsessions. Certainly part of the appeal of the past is that it can be manipulated, toyed with, and offers no resistance. It can similarly be shrouded beneath layers of obfuscation, indefinitely sustaining its fascination. But the most obvious explanation is fortuitous timing. Tanizaki was able, through one of those quirks of kismet, to achieve a unity between his aesthetic and personal tastes at this point in life. No sooner had he begun a serious study of Japanese tradition (while still fired by his thirst for its exotic appeal) than he met a woman who came to embody many of the finest virtues of that tradition. It is pointless to attempt to analyze whether this woman was truly an embodiment of the Japanese past (there are, after all, sufficient indications that she was truly modern as well[63])—the point is that Tanizaki began to worship her as the ideal woman, and that the trappings of adoration in which he adorned his new Galatea were derived from his concurrent absorption in traditional Japanese culture.

It was probably in February of 1927 that Tanizaki first met Nezu Matsuko.[64] By this time Tanizaki was not only a well-known and controversial author; he was also on his way to becoming a very rich one.[65] A Japanese publisher had begun issuing a landmark series of modern Japanese fiction, selling at one-yen per volume. Tanizaki's was the third of sixty-three volumes published, and the accessibility of contemporary writings which the series offered to a rapidly expanding reading audience made many writers wealthy. To celebrate the inauguration of the series, the publisher invited writers like Akutagawa and Satō to come to Osaka to give public lectures. After the lectures were concluded, Tanizaki and Chiyo joined Mr. and Mrs. Satō (Satō and Tanizaki had patched up their friendship a year or so earlier, and Satō had married a former geisha) and Akutagawa at a performance of the puppet theater. During this interval of partying, Tanizaki and Akutagawa were invited to a celebration sponsored by Nezu Matsuko. Her husband, Seitarō, was one of the wealthiest merchants in Osaka, the owner of a cotton wholesaler's that had been in business for 300 years. Though Seitarō had married Matsuko, a famous beauty, in 1924, and had given her everything money could buy, he held back a portion of his wealth and affection to lavish upon other women as well. He liked to fancy himself a patron of the arts, and he surrounded himself with famous writers and painters as a symbol of his power. It was to such a gathering that Tanizaki and Akutagawa were invited.[66] There is some irony in the fact that Seitarō, in an attempt to legitimize his own social position, should bring into his circle a writer to whom he would end up losing his wife.

Matsuko was the second daughter of a wealthy stockholder in a major shipbuilding company. All four daughters were renowned for their beauty and cultural accomplishments. (Readers who like to jump ahead in their thinking will already have identified the women who served as models for *The Makioka Sisters*.) Although she and Seitarō had been blessed with two children, she was unhappy with his profligacy,[67] and would eventually spend much of her time living apart. After meeting Tanizaki and Akutagawa, she invited the two men to the Union dance hall, where Tanizaki's lessons from a Russian tutor a few years earlier came in handy. He decked himself out in a tuxedo, Akutagawa fastening the studs. In typical romantic fashion, Tanizaki and Matsuko danced the night away in each other's arms.[68]

The blossoming romance did not immediately bear fruit, however: Tanizaki first had to divorce Chiyo and then marry and divorce another woman before his indistinct image of Matsuko would congeal into a vision of the ideal woman. His major preoccupation in 1927 was a famed debate on the nature of fiction with his good friend, Akutagawa Ryūnosuke. This was to be the final year of Akutagawa's short life, and his attitudes toward literature had changed dramatically since his debut several years earlier as a creator of almost Gothic-like fiction. Akutagawa began to contend in print that the "story" in a work of literature was of little artistic consequence. For such a skilled "story"-teller, this seemed an odd statement, and Tanizaki responded, in an essay of his own, that he found it inordinately difficult to assess the artistic value of the "story-less" stories with a "poetic spirit" for which Akutagawa claimed superiority. He wrote: "Of late I have developed the bad habit of being interested only in what is untrue.... I am sure that truthful stories are also valid, but in recent years I have come to prefer the devious to the straightforward and the noxious to the innocuous; and I like complicated things that are embellished with maximum intricacy."[69] Such is a description not only of Tanizaki's literary art, but of the intimate relationships in his life. In his defense of plot, Tanizaki argued: "Plot interest is ... the way in which a work is assembled, interest in structure, architectural beauty. It cannot be said that this is without artistic value.... It is of course not the sole value, but I myself believe that among the literary forms the novel is that which can possess the greatest sense of structural beauty. To do away with plot interest is to throw away the special prerogatives of the form known as the novel."[70] Akutagawa gave an uncharacteristically restrained response to Tanizaki's arguments in June, and the following month, citing in a note the "indistinct anxiety" that perpetually tormented him, Akutagawa committed suicide.[71]

In 1928 Tanizaki began serialization of two of his most important novels: *Manji* (Maelstrom)[72] and *Tade kuu mushi* (Some Prefer Nettles; trans. 1955). *Nettles* was one of the few novels that Tanizaki undertook without preparing a detailed outline in advance.[73] It scarcely needed an outline, however, since it was clearly derived from Tanizaki's own relationship with Chiyo, his boredom with her though she was a good woman, and his hesitation at severing the relationship until he had a new object of adulation to pursue. The novel is one of the most concise and intriguing studies of infatuation in

Japanese literature. With remarkable self-awareness, Tanizaki describes the indistinct shifting of his hero Kaname's interests away from the thinly veneered Westernization of his wife, Misako; the intermediate journey through ambivalence in his affair with a "Eurasian" prostitute, Louise; and the final focusing of his intellectual and physical passions on the doll-like mistress of his father-in-law, the traditional Ohisa. It is probably no coincidence that Tanizaki's encounters with Matsuko were growing more frequent as he composed this novel. He and Chiyo began the study of *jiuta*, a traditional form of folk singing, early in 1929, and in July they were both invited to Matsuko's home, where along with Matsuko and her sisters they began practicing the dances that accompany the *jiuta*. On New Year's Day in 1930, a performance was held at Tanizaki's home. Matsuko rendered the "*Kurokami*" (Jet-black Hair) number, a folk song that seems to reverberate with the feelings that she and Tanizaki had for one another: ·

It is the pillow
We shared that night,
When I let down
My jet-black hair.
That is the cause of my lament
When I sleep alone
With my single robe
To cover me.
"You are mine," he said,
Not knowing the heart
Of a simple girl.
The voice of a temple bell
Sounds into the quiet night.
Awakening from an empty dream
In the morning,
How lovely, sweet,
And helpless is my longing.
Before I know it
The silver snow has piled up.[74]

Remove Chiyo from the picture and you have a scene that

could have come directly from *The Makioka Sisters*. And that
is precisely the next step Tanizaki took—removing Chiyo
from the picture. One of the most remarkable games of Tanizaki's life was played out that summer. Satō Haruo, who had
concluded that his relationship with his geisha wife had turned
irrevocably stale, decided to divorce her, and had done so by
the middle of June. Putting that problem behind him, Satō
went to Kansai to spend some time with his close friends, the
Tanizakis, and salve his wounds. "Then, half in jest," Satō has
written, "I told Tanizaki that the next time I wanted a wife
with tender feelings who came from Kansai. Tanizaki turned
serious and remarked, 'Well, what do you think—do you feel
like marrying Chiyo? If you do, it would help me a great deal
as well. To be honest, I've had this secret wish for some
time....' I didn't give him an immediate answer."

Satō, quite certain that Chiyo no longer cared for him as
she had ten years earlier at the time of the Odawara incident,
decided to relay the peculiar conversation to Chiyo. Over the
next few days, the three of them, in different configurations
(rather like the whirling of a "maelstrom," one might say),
continued to discuss the possibilities. Initially Chiyo's response was negative, so Satō returned to Tokyo, but later
wrote a letter that apparently elicited a deep-felt response. By
July 14 Satō was back at the Tanizakis', and around the twen-
ty-third Chiyo announced that she would leave the details of
the swap to Tanizaki and Satō.[75] The next day, Tanizaki sat
down with their daughter, Ayuko, who was then fourteen, to
attempt an explanation of what was going to happen.[76] Early
in August, the trio journeyed together to make their plans
known to Satō's family. Then, on August 18, they mailed out
announcements under their three signatures to friends and relatives. After a conventional opening, the notice read:

> Recently the three of us have met together, and we have
> mutually agreed that Chiyo will divorce Jun'ichirō and marry
> Haruo. Jun'ichirō's daughter, Ayuko, will be able to live with
> her mother. Naturally, associations between all parties will

continue as before. Given these circumstances, we pray that your solicitude toward us will but increase. At the earliest opportunity we will engage a go-between and hold a formal reception, but for the time being we send you this brief announcement by way of notification.[77]

In a telephone interview from his home, Tanizaki commented on his feelings toward Chiyo: "She was my wife for sixteen years. She had no particular faults as a woman, but with my nature being as it is, there were some aspects of her personality that just didn't suit mine."[78] This peculiar affair fascinated some, scandalized others. In his journal entry for August 20, Nagai Kafū recorded: "Today something came from Tanizaki. It was so funny, I'll record it below," and he proceeds to copy out the tripartite announcement. But the Catholic school for girls that Ayuko attended was not amused and expelled her.

Tanizaki felt it was only proper that he move from the house, but he was determined to remain in the Kansai area. Mrs. Nezu helped him find a place to live while the details of the divorce were being worked out. He secluded himself away for a month and wrote "*Yoshinokuzu*" (Arrowroot; trans. 1982), which, together with *Some Prefer Nettles*, Tanizaki cited as among his favorite works.[79] It is the kind of layered work he delighted in composing during this "middle" period—combining a modern character who delves into the past, yearnings for a lost mother, and legends from his childhood such as folktales concerning fox spirits. This absorption with the past did not, however, mean that he was romantically idle. A series of love letters discovered in 1986 intimate that Tanizaki had grown enamored of a woman who served in his house for about a year beginning in the fall of 1928. The letters suggest that Tanizaki may have been thinking of marrying the woman, but the whole plan was jettisoned when Chiyo found out about it. Tanizaki's final letter to the woman was sent just four days before the divorce/swap announcement.[80] Meanwhile (one supposes, though perhaps simultaneously),

Tanizaki had not abandoned his youthful hope of marrying one of the stunning waitresses at the Kairakuen restaurant. Just after his divorce from Chiyo, he traveled up to Tokyo to discuss with Sasanuma's wife the possibilities of marrying one particular waitress. He was startled to learn that the woman had married a few days earlier.

Never long daunted in such matters, by January of 1931 Tanizaki was engaged to marry yet another woman, Furukawa Tomiko. At twenty-four years, she was only slightly more than half his age. She held a degree in English literature from Osaka Women's College, and during her student years she had begun to call on Tanizaki regularly for literary instruction. She had also assisted him in making translations into Japanese of Thomas Hardy's "Barbara of the House of Grebe" and Stendhal's "The Abbess of Castro" (which he never completed). Tanizaki was able to get her a job on the editorial staff of a magazine published by the *Bungei Shunjū*. The marriage took place on April 24.

It is difficult to understand why Tanizaki bothered with this marriage. Even while on his honeymoon with Tomiko on Mount Kōya, his affections were inclining toward another woman—Nezu Matsuko, of course—and by the end of 1932 he and Tomiko had separated. He wrote "*Mōmoku monogatari*" (A Blind Man's Tale; trans. 1963) while secluded on the Buddhist holy mountain, and confessed later that it was indeed Matsuko who had been his inspiration for the work (even the illustration of the female protagonist in the frontispiece had Matsuko as its model). His contacts with Matsuko grew more frequent. The most interesting of these came just after his marriage to Tomiko (the second Mrs. Tanizaki): the newlyweds joined Satō Haruo and his wife (the first Mrs. Tanizaki) and Matsuko (eventually to be Mrs. Tanizaki number three) to view the blossoms at the Dōjōji Temple (the setting, one might point out, for a Nō play about a vengeful woman who transforms herself into a serpent). Such experiences help to explain Tanizaki's fascination with *The Tale of Genji*, that wonderful classical tale of quasi-polygamous liaisons and women who congregate around the Shining Prince with the full knowledge that they have all been his lovers at one time or another—or simultaneously. Often they are women who resemble Genji's late mother.

For a time, the newly (and briefly) wed couple stayed in a dormitory belonging to Matsuko's husband's company, then moved from there into a cottage owned by Matsuko's family. The fateful move came in the spring of 1932, when the Tanizakis took a house next door to Matsuko. She would come over from time to time to perform a *jiuta* dance, and her elegance and beauty undoubtedly had a profound affect on Tanizaki. At the beginning of that summer he told her that he worshiped the ground she tread on (leading some critics to speculate that Matsuko, unlike his first two wives, was willing to satisfy, in imagination if not in fact, Tanizaki's desire to be treated cruelly[81]). Though flattered, she responded that she did not wish to hurt Tomiko. Almost two years of tantalizing agony would pass before Tanizaki and Matsuko began living together.

That period of personal torment inspired some of Tanizaki's most exquisite literature. He completed the serialization of one his most grotesque masterpieces, *Bushūkō hiwa* (The Secret History of the Lord of Musashi; trans. 1982); ran a series of delightful articles on Osaka and its inhabitants, which more than obliquely suggest that his attraction to the culture of Kansai had its roots in his yearning for his childhood ("When such a person as I walks the streets of a city in the Kansai, he is overcome with nostalgia for his own childhood. Today the plebeian flatlands [*shitamachi*] of Tokyo have lost the last vestiges of their former appearance, but sometimes, in an old part of Kyoto or Osaka, you come upon rows of the same heavy-roofed houses, the same latticed fronts. You say to yourself, as if remembering your long-forgotten home, 'Ah, Tokyo was once like this!'"[82]); published two of what could arguably be the finest novellas in modern Japanese fiction:

Ashikari (trans. 1936) and *Shunkin-shō* (A Portrait of Shunkin; trans. 1963); and penned his ultimate paean to traditional Japanese aesthetic values, *In'ei raisan* (In Praise of Shadows; trans. 1977).

In Praise of Shadows is a key work to understanding the aesthetic preferences that would sustain Tanizaki from this period until the end of his career. Those preferences, at least as he expressed them in their idealized form, are markedly different from his tastes of twenty years earlier. Where he had described the ideal woman from his days of infatuation with the West as shapely and certainly best viewed in bright illumination, in this essay he recalls his mother and overlaps her image with those of a statue of Kannon, the Buddhist goddess of mercy, and with Japanese women in general from former days:

> The chest as flat as a board, breasts paper-thin, back, hips, and buttocks forming an undeviating straight line, the whole body so lean and gaunt as to seem out of proportion with the face, hands, and feet, so lacking in substance as to give the impression not of flesh but of a stick—must not the traditional Japanese woman have had just such a physique?...
>
> I suppose it is hard for those who praise the fleshly beauty we see under today's bright lights to imagine the ghostly beauty of those older women. And there may be some who argue that if beauty has to hide its weak points in the dark it is not beauty at all. But we Orientals, as I have suggested before, create a kind of beauty of the shadows we have made in out-of-the-way places.... We find beauty not in the thing itself but in the pattern of shadows, the light and the darkness, that one thing against another creates.
>
> A phosphorescent jewel gives off its glow and color in the dark and loses its beauty in the light of day. Were it not for shadows, there would be no beauty. Our ancestors made of woman an object inseparable from darkness, like lacquerware decorated in gold or mother-of-pearl. They hid as much of her as they could in shadows, concealing her arms and legs in the folds of long sleeves and skirts, so that one part and one only stood out—her face. The curveless body may, by comparison

with Western women, be ugly. But our thoughts do not travel
to what we cannot see. The unseen for us does not exist. The
person who insists upon seeing her ugliness, like the person
who would shine a hundred-candlepower light upon the picture alcove, drives away whatever beauty may reside there.[83]

These aesthetic tastes are, of course, more Tanizaki's than
those of men of the past. But Tanizaki advances his personal
views so persuasively and so eloquently that it seems only
natural to embrace them as authentic. *In Praise of Shadows*
ranges widely in its subject matter: it goes on at length about
conventional Japanese toilets with their mixture of dark cubi-
cles and dusky smells, about food, the color of Japanese skin,
works of art, and the "ideal" Japanese house. The fact that
Tanizaki much preferred to write about his ideals than to live
them is beautifully expressed in an ironic story related by
Matsuko after Tanizaki's death. On one of the many occasions
when Tanizaki was having a new house built, he summoned
the architect to discuss what he wanted. The clever architect,
hoping to stroke his famous client's pride, said he knew precisely what kind of house Tanizaki wanted: he had read *In
Praise of Shadows*. "Oh, no," Tanizaki groaned, "I could
never live in a house like that!"[84]

The world of darkness and shadows—a world not unlike
the realm of concealed sexual idiosyncrasies that he had described in his earlier writings—is central to his masterpieces
of this period, the works inspired by his craving for Matsuko.
Shadowy settings, hidden motivations, actual and metaphori-
cal blindness, the intentional confusion of one character with
another—all these elements fill the pages of *Ashikari* and *Portrait of Shunkin*. It is tempting to call *Shunkin* a perfectly
crafted work, with its antiquarian narrator examining ques-
tionable historical "evidence" about the complex relationship
between the samisen master Shunkin and her submissive disciple, Sasuke. Tanizaki's narrative style has abandoned the
aggressive authoritarian stance of his early stories, and is
much more like the almost disembodied narrators of classical

Tanizaki in his later years.

Tanizaki around the age
of five, 1890.

Tanizaki's mother, Seki,
in her fifties.

Classmates and teachers at Sakamoto Primary School (Tanizaki in
middle at back, Mr. Inaba second from left in front, and Sasanuma
Gennosuke at far right).

Tanizaki at Rokkō Hotel in
Hyogo Prefecture, 1924.

Tanizaki in 1928.

Nezu Matsuko (the third Mrs. Tanizaki) and her sisters, who served
as models for *The Makioka Sisters*.

Tanizaki and Shiga Naoya immediately after the war.

Tanizaki at his writing desk.

monogatari tales. He had in fact written that "We Japanese writers find it increasingly tiresome to write dialogue as we advance in years; we tend to choose the *monogatari* form over the novel, and in the end, as we abridge even the narrative and grow weary of building scenes, we favor the drier elegance of the essay style."[85] Such a depersonalized narrative stance allows for an abundance of ambiguity, for the creation of gaping black holes into which the reader's imagination is forced to descend. What the reader chooses to discover there is a matter of personal prerogative. Once the reader has joined Tanizaki's game in the dark, there are almost no limits imposed on the imagination. It is possible, for instance, to read the work *Shunkin* as an elaborate game: the twists and turns in the story, against all surface meaning, make it feasible that it was Sasuke himself who broke into Shunkin's room and splashed boiling water on her face; that he then, with impunity, drove needles into his own eyes in order to join her in the world of eternal blackness. Sasuke's life becomes one of "complete happiness ... for in his dark, sensual world the eternal and the fleeting, life and art ... are perfectly united."[86] Sometimes startling discovers are made in the dark.

In the spring of 1934 Tanizaki and Matsuko brought their relationship out of the shadows and began to live openly together. Matsuko brought along her eldest daughter and later her son. Her divorce from Seitarō was finalized in April, Tanizaki's from Tomiko in October. The couple were married on January 28, 1935, at Tanizaki's house. It was the fulfillment of a lifelong dream, and as if in celebration of the unification of his life and art, Tanizaki turned his prodigious talents to a modern re-creation of the most important literary text in Japan, a work brimming with the aesthetics of shadows, remarkable for its idealization of a maternal figure, and riddled with confusion of character—*The Tale of Genji*.

The idea to translate *Genji* into an accessible modern idiom (many Japanese of the twentieth century, irretrievably removed from the language of eleventh-century Japan, were more comfortable reading the work in Arthur Waley's English translation) came from Tanizaki's editor at the Chūō Kōron publishing company. The notion was initially daunting, but with assurances that he would have expert help from scholars who had dedicated their lives to the tale, Tanizaki began this labor of love with full vigor. It would consume virtually all his creative energies for the next three years. The only work of original fiction he would produce between 1935 and 1941 was the delightful *Neko to Shōzō to futari no onna* (A Cat, a Man, and Two Women, 1936; trans. 1990), which, as its translator suggests, may have been Tanizaki's attempt to keep in contact with the "humbler, more quotidian reality"[87] of the common man in Osaka as he himself became increasingly absorbed in the elegant world of the Heian court.

The first of twenty-six volumes in *The Tale of Genji as Translated by Jun'ichirō*, as it was titled, began to appear in January of 1939, six months after the outbreak of war with China. Because the cult of emperor worship was being bolstered to rally the people for the war effort, the portions of *Genji* that dealt with illegitimate succession in the imperial family (Genji's shadowy affair with the Emperor's consort, a woman who closely resembles his own late mother) were excised from Tanizaki's translation.

In April of that year, completing the intricate knot linking Tanizaki's family with that of Satō Haruo, Tanizaki's only child, his daughter Ayuko, married a nephew of Satō's. Shortly thereafter, as if to put familial relations aside once and for all, Matsuko submitted to an abortion.[88] They would have no children of their own.

In July of 1941, when the final volume of his *Genji* appeared, the event was celebrated publicly by his election to the Japan Academy of Art, which had been formed that year. Nonetheless, Tanizaki's wartime literary activities were greatly circumscribed. In fact, the two writers who were able to remain aloof from the war effort were Tanizaki and his old mentor, Nagai Kafū. Tanizaki's cooperation with the propaganda authorities was limited to the authoring of one radio script on the fall of Singapore and a handful of poems that express not support for the war but concern over what will happen to Japan,[89] and he allowed himself to be made an "honorary member" of the Japanese Literature Patriotic Association. Unlike most writers of the war years, however, Tanizaki did not produce jingoistic works praising the heroism of Japanese soldiers, nor did he travel to occupied territories to lecture on the superior virtues of Japanese culture. Tanizaki's longstanding hatred for the military[90] was reinforced in his mind early in 1943. The previous spring he had moved into a new house in Atami and there began composition of *Sasameyuki* (The Makioka Sisters; trans. 1957). The first two installments were carried in *Chūō Kōron* in January and March of 1943, but to the surprise of Tanizaki's dedicated readers, no episode appeared in the May issue, and the following month a notice was published in the magazine which stated: "Having taken into consideration the possibility that this novel might exert an undesirable influence, in view of present exigencies at this decisive stage of the war, we have regretfully decided from the standpoint of self-discipline to discontinue further publication."[91] Tanizaki had been censored many times before, but never for a work so innocuous and so "traditional" in nature.

In July of 1944, the military ordered Chūō Kōron and several other commercial publishers to suspend operations altogether. The response by Tanizaki was privately to put out the first part of *The Makioka Sisters* in a limited edition of 200 copies, financed with his own funds and some money contributed by Chūō Kōron. Even this irritated the military censors, and Tanizaki was ordered to publish no more of the novel. Although he had completed the second part by the end of 1944, he released no more of it until after the end of the war. A shared loathing of the military brought Tanizaki and Kafū even closer together, and they exchanged frequent visits. Both were concerned that the war would do irreparable damage to the traditional culture they so loved. When Kafū learned that he would no longer be able to obtain writing brushes made of bristles imported from China, he grumbled, "The collapse of Japanese civilization is at hand."[92] To comfort his friend, Tanizaki sent Kafū a parcel containing scissors, a knife, an inkpad, over a thousand sheets of writing paper, a yukata, and a stiff obi. Kafū records that he was barely able to hold back the tears of gratitude.[93]

Less than two months after the end of the war, even before he had made preparations to move his family from their place of refuge in Atami back to Kansai, Tanizaki had traveled to Tokyo to make plans to publish further chapters of *The Makioka Sisters*. He spent the first several months of 1946 finding a house in Kyoto and settling in, then resumed his work on the novel. Both Tanizaki and Kafū had become something on the order of national cultural heroes after the defeat because of their refusal to cooperate with the military, and a series of public honors were bestowed on them. A few months after publishing the second part of *The Makioka Sisters*, Tanizaki was invited to the Kyoto Imperial Palace along with several other writers, and they held a discussion of Japanese literature in the presence of Emperor Hirohito. In November of that year, before the novel was even completed, it received the first Culture Prize from the Mainichi Publishing group; less than a month after the finished work appeared in print at the end of 1948, it was awarded the Asahi Culture Prize. In March of 1949 he was invited to dine with the Emperor, and in November he joined Shiga Naoya in being awarded the Medal of Culture, the highest honor which the Japanese government can bestow upon an artist.

The Makioka Sisters is, as virtually every reader has acknowledged, a masterpiece, as placid, controlled, and beautiful as Tanizaki's early stories were frenetic, reckless, and distasteful. Although the narrator of the work is essentially a cipher, Tanizaki brings his considerable energy as a storyteller to the seemingly impossible task of imposing order and aesthetic beauty (primarily of the traditional type) onto his tale while the world around him is engaged in the self-destructive activities of war. To a large extent, *The Makioka Sisters* is about a family making every possible effort to stay the deleterious effects of changing times. The sisters' absorption in the various rituals of daily life, as well as the regular observance of public festivities such as the viewing of cherry blossoms and the chasing of fireflies, help them retain a sense of unity and continuity when all the forces at work on the family—economic decline, early intimations of international war, Taeko's rebellious behavior, the paradoxical quest (paradoxical in that it will mean separation from the family) to find a husband for Yukiko—threaten to tear it apart. Tanizaki's success in this "novel of manners" is extraordinary, and he provides his readers with as intimate and loving a portrait of a Japanese family as can be found in any work of literature. It is likely that many readers will finish the novel feeling they know these four sisters more fully and more affectionately than they know any real-life Japanese family.

The novel is perhaps the strongest evidence that Tanizaki had rid himself of his fleeting infatuations with modernity, and with love as well. The sustained mood of calm nostalgia is new for him, and it is a most welcome stance. Not that *The Makioka Sisters* is without its shadows (though it seems to be without its fetishes and perversions). Yukiko is a complex figure, wielding far more control through passive means than she is often given credit for. Ferociously stubborn when she has to be, frustratingly silent when she chooses, firmly outspoken when the occasion demands—the overall impression is that she allows circumstances to develop as they will, so long as things turn out ultimately as she likes. In that sense, she is the *sasameyuki* of the title; the customary (literal) translation is "thin snow," but it is a snow that falls thick and fast and covers the ground, staying longer than its fragile appearance would suggest; much like Yukiko herself.[94]

Unlike some of the older "deans" of Japanese literature who chose to rest upon their prewar laurels and bask in public acclaim after the war without producing any new, significant works of literature, Tanizaki remained active, even startling so, virtually to the end of his life. Although high blood pressure began to plague him as early as the spring of 1947, Tanizaki pressed on with his work. No sooner had he completed *The Makioka Sisters* than he was talking with an Osaka newspaper about the serialization of a new novel. Initially this work was intended as a sequel to *The Secret History of the Lord of Musashi*, which Tanizaki had wanted to write as early as 1933.[95] But after his immersion in *Genji*, it was the Heian period rather than the medieval warrior days that tugged at his imagination, and the work he began serializing in December of 1949 was another quest for a mother, *Shōshō Shigemoto no haha* (The Mother of Captain Shigemoto), a work yet untranslated which many Japanese scholars considered the finest distillation of his varied literary motifs.

Although his work was little affected by his age and declining health (he wrote *The Mother of Captain Shigemoto* in almost record time[96]), there are indications that he was beginning to feel the discrepancy in age between himself and Matsuko (she was seventeen years younger). As he was writing *Shigemoto*, he spoke to her about his anxieties and gave her permission, if she were so inclined, to have an affair with another man to satisfy her passions. This pronouncement takes on added significance when one considers that Tanizaki at the same time produced the outline for a novel dealing with an aging scholar who encourages his young wife to take a lover, then voyeuristically pores over her diary so that he can share in their amorous games by proxy. That novel, *Kagi* (The Key), would not be published until 1956.

Once again in 1950, Tanizaki threw his full energies into a revision of his translation of *The Tale of Genji*. He took advantage of new work by scholars of classical literature, and altered the language of his first translation to make it more colloquial in tone. That "new translation" was published in twelve volumes between May of 1951 and December of 1954.

Shortly after it began to appear, Tanizaki received another prestigious honor from his country—he was given the Order of Cultural Merit. Meanwhile, though he was producing no original fiction of his own, Tanizaki's earlier writings were being made available to an expanded audience on the stage and screen. Film and stage adaptations of *The Makioka Sisters*, *Shigemoto*,[97] *Ashikari*, and even a dramatic version of his *Genji* translation were produced for admiring viewers.

The battle against high blood pressure continued, and in May of 1953 his eyes began to trouble him, so Tanizaki hired a scribe to take dictation for a time. After completing his second *Genji*, Tanizaki felt compelled to take a fond look back at his own childhood once again, this time not in the form of fiction but in a delightful memoir, *Yōshō jidai* (Childhood Years; trans. 1990), which captures much of the mood and tempo of late nineteenth-century Tokyo. This was followed by the serialization of *The Key*, which created such a stir because of its explicit eroticism and voyeurism that it became an item of debate in the legal affairs subcommittee of the Japanese Diet. Readers, however, were fascinated that a seventy-year-old man could retain such a virile interest in sexual relations, and the issues of *Chūō Kōron* in which the novel appeared were instant sell-outs. In his preface to the German translation, Henry Miller wrote that Tanizaki was the most masculine writer of the twentieth century.[98]

The next serious blow to Tanizaki's health came in November of 1958. He was sitting down to write out a congratulatory message to his childhood friend and benefactor, Sasanuma Gennosuke, on the occasion of his golden wedding anniversary, when his right hand became paralyzed. Several months of rest did not restore it to use, so the following year Tanizaki once again engaged a scribe to take down his work as he spoke it. This was the process Tanizaki used to compose "The Bridge of Dreams" in the fall of 1959, and the complex associations of character and plot which traverse the dream-like landscape of the story make the circumstances of its writing all the more remarkable. As in *The Makioka Sisters*, the presence of *The Tale of Genji* as a powerful subtext is evident in this story, with its confusion of mother and stepmother, the incestuous relationship between the teenaged narrator and his "surrogate" mother, and the child born to them who is passed off as the son of the narrator's father.

Tanizaki and Matsuko celebrated their silver wedding anniversary in July of 1960. Three months later, Tanizaki suffered a heart attack, and spent the next two months in a hospital. While he was bedridden, Sasanuma Gennosuke died of cancer, and two of his other closest friends passed away that same year. His health stabilized after his discharge from the hospital, and in May of 1962 he published the coda to his literary oeuvre, a masterpiece of elderly eroticism titled *Fūten rōjin nikki* (Diary of a Mad Old Man; trans. 1965). A second heart attack came in the summer of 1963.

These recurring reminders of his mortality, however, did nothing to dim the literary immortality that was surging around Tanizaki's name. Translations of most of his major novels had begun to appear in many languages in the mid-1950s, and international prestige followed. In May of 1964 Tanizaki became the first Japanese selected as an honorary member of the American Academy and Institute of Arts and Letters, and his name began to be mentioned with increasing fervency as a candidate for the Nobel Prize in Literature. Speculation about such matters is fruitless, but it does seem likely that he would have received the prize had he still been alive when Japan's "turn" came around. But even as he was commencing work on a "new, revised" translation of *Genji* in postwar *kana*-usage (the last of ten volumes appeared three months after his death), his health took a turn for the worse with the enlargement of his prostate. In January of 1965 he had surgery to remove a urinary obstruction, and in July he suffered a kidney attack. On the thirtieth of that month his heart gave out, and Tanizaki was dead.

There are good indications that Tanizaki had no pretensions about his own writings. He once wrote that, "I was basically uninterested in politics, so I concerned myself exclusively with the ways people live, eat and dress, the standards of feminine beauty, and the progress of recreational facilities."[99] And there will always be those critics who castigate him for his supposed lack of intellectual substance. There can be no doubt, however, of the significance and power of Tanizaki's probings into the shadows of human appetite, and his discovery that human beings are not as overwhelmingly controlled by sterile reason as we would like to pretend. The games he initiates in the dark are overtly sexual, but they spill over into the manner of his narration, which, in many ways, is also a complex game between author and reader. Tanizaki often presents us with unreliable narrators who wave spurious historical documents in our faces in a deliberate attempt to confound us. They manipulate facts to their own advantage, form unsupported conclusions, but provide us with no means to argue against them. To read Tanizaki is to be forced (again the sadomasochistic relation between author and reader appears) to rely upon the imagination set free, for there is nothing of substance to hold onto otherwise. It is for that boundless imagination, for that perverse refusal to live the kind of life or write the kind of fiction that convention demanded, for that gleeful absorption in one infatuation after another, that Tanizaki will be best and most fondly remembered.

But perhaps most important of all the facets of Tanizaki's work is the shift in his personal affections from the West to traditional Japan, for that is a "conversion" played out in the lives of many modern Japanese, whether bohemian writers or blue-suited businessmen. As early as 1915, he could write:

> I discovered that, as a modern Japanese, there were fierce artistic desires burning within me that could not be satisfied when I was surrounded by Japanese. Unfortunately for me, I could no longer find anything in present-day Japan, the land of my birth, which answered my craving for beauty.... I

would have to seek from the West objects to satisfy my craving for beauty, and I was suddenly overcome with passionate
admiration for the West.... I felt an uncontrollable desire to
learn everything there was to be known about the countries of
Europe that have given birth to these many astonishing works
of art, and about the various aspects of the daily lives of the
superior race of men living there. Everything labeled as coming from the West seemed beautiful and aroused my envy. I
could not help looking at the West in the same way that
human beings look up to the gods.... I made up my mind that
the only way to develop my art fully was to come into ever
closer contact with the West, if only by an inch closer than
before, or even by totally assimilating myself into the West.[100]

It is interesting to note Tanizaki's feverish description of
his mood: "craving ... passionate admiration ... uncontrollable desire ... beautiful ... aroused my envy ... by totally assimilating myself...." These are words that seem as suited to
the initial stages of a romantic affair as to an infatuation with a
foreign culture. Viewed as an extension of Tanizaki's own
emotional leanings, his fascination with the West becomes
more comprehensible, as does his ultimate decision to put that
youthful crush behind him and embrace a mature love. Ironically, it seems that what attracted him most about traditional
Japanese culture was that it reminded him of his childhood
and his relationship with his mother. That is true of virtually
every aspect of his adoration of tradition, whether it be his
long-term professional involvement with *The Tale of Genji* or
his aesthetic views about toilets: "A certain nostalgic sweet re-
membrance accompanies the smell of a toilet. For example,
when someone who has been away from home a long time returns after an absence of years, when he goes into the toilet
and smells the odor he knew long ago, it brings back better
than anything else warm memories of his younger days, and
he really feels the warmth of 'I'm home!'"[101] The passions and
cravings of earlier days have been replaced by "warm ...
sweet ... nostalgic" smells of a home that cannot be retrieved
except in the dark recesses of memory. That retrieval may en-

tail the fantasy of an incestuous embrace of mother that brings the adult full circle in the course of his life, but one cannot deny the incredible and enduring beauty of the shape that nostalgia took in Tanizaki's greatest work, *The Makioka Sisters*. The yearnings in Tanizaki's writings, whether erotic or nostalgic, are the yearnings of every human being.

A Detachment from Modernity
Kawabata Yasunari

My first encounter with Japanese fiction was the English translation of Kawabata Yasunari's *Snow Country*, shortly after Kawabata became the first and, thus far, the only Japanese writer to receive the Nobel Prize in Literature. As a newcomer to Japan, I had high expectations that the works of an internationally recognized author would help me close the gap between myself and my unfamiliar surroundings. Initially, at least, the crisp descriptions of the snowy setting in northern Japan, the vivid evocations of hot springs resorts, the examination of the life of a geisha with its attendant laxness of morals—all these elements persuaded me that, as I dug into the novel, my understanding of Japan was deepening, the distance I felt from Japanese culture narrowing.

Before long, though, I began to feel uncomfortable around Shimamura, the male protagonist. It was a feeling of uneasiness I had not experienced in the presence of many Western fictional heroes. I thought perhaps it was his inability—or unwillingness?—to drop all the emotional barriers between himself and his vibrant lover, Komako, that had turned me against him. After all, she was a genuine, open, appealing woman who seemed more than willing to share herself fully with Shimamura and develop their relationship to the furthest boundaries of intimacy.

But then came what purported to be the "ending" of the story, when the Milky Way came rushing down into Shima-mura's heart. Frantically I flipped the page over, looking for the continuation of the human drama, certain that there had to be more. But the next page only recommended "other works of modern Japanese fiction you won't want to miss." I felt cheated, angry, bewildered. I had invested some emotional stakes of my own in these two people, and someone—Shima-mura? Kawabata? the book bindery?—had cheated me of a resolution of their relationship. And what in the devil did the Milky Way have to do with anything?

Admittedly my initial reading of modern Japanese fiction was lacking in sophistication, in cultural background, in sensitivity. But subsequent readings of Kawabata have only confirmed my initial sense that while his works may be filled with human characters, they are curiously lacking in human relationships; that the closer I try to draw to the individuals who people his fiction, the more conscious I become of the barriers of distance that Kawabata erects around them, and of the strong, almost polarized forces of resistance that continually push his characters away from involvement and toward isolation. I have, certainly, come to see such a feature of his work not as some flaw in his literary creativity, but as a crucial part of what his writing is all about. And central to understanding this stance of detachment and distancing in his work is the recognition that it was also a dominating feature of his own life.

In an interestingly self-revelatory work that he published in 1934, Kawabata wrote: "I feel as though I have never yet held a woman's hand in a romantic sense. There may be some women who will accuse me of lying. But I have the feeling that this is no mere figure of speech. And is it not true that it is not only the hands of women that I have never held? Is that not also true of life for me? Is it not also true of reality? And perhaps even of literature? Am I a happy man deserving of pity?"[1]

By 1934 Kawabata had in his stock of memories two painful love affairs from his youth—one homosexual, the other with a fifteen-year-old girl who jilted him—and had been married for eight years. With this quotation, then, as with much of his writing about himself, we must be careful not to take him too literally. Because this remark comes in the midst of a "literary" autobiography, it must be regarded as a lyrical expression of Kawabata's feelings about his life. The issue here is not that he has never had sexual relations with a woman, but that the distance he felt in all his relationships—his associations with women, with men, with life, reality, and with literature—had kept him from experiencing that interchange of intimate emotions that marks the passage from youth into adulthood, from innocence into maturity, from isolation into love. Although Kawabata the man associated closely with several people in his personal life, it is as though he remained an emotional virgin. Though Kawabata the writer actively participated in all manner of literary groups, journal staffs, prize juries, and discussion meetings, he seems never to have removed the final layer of self-protection that would topple the walls he built around himself. To appropriate a current colloquialism, Kawabata practiced "safe sex"—that is, protected and shielded himself—in every relationship of his life. Whether he was driven by a fear of closeness, the "orphan's disposition" that he and his critics cite so frequently, by an inherent aloofness, or by some other complex mixture of motives, Kawabata must ultimately be seen as a man who, as a child, was isolated by the successive deaths of all his relatives, and who, as a man, chose to maintain his separation from others in his life and writings. By the time of the defeat of Japan in 1945, Kawabata had even come to feel detached from the modern world in which he lived, and though he would persist in writing about his contemporaries, his subject matter became in essence the loss of human ties and the irretrievable beauty of the past. Perhaps only an individual like Kawabata would have thought to combine the two words "beauty" and "sadness" in the title of one of his last novels.

For all the emphasis that will be placed on Kawabata's detachment from the key elements of existence in the life story that unfolds below, it is important to remember how fondly his associates and friends thought of him; how kind and considerate he was toward literary friend and literary foe alike; how diligently he labored to bring the talents of new writers—often isolated outcasts themselves—to the attention of the literary world; how vital a role he played, as president of the Japan PEN Club for seventeen years, in creating an international reading audience for modern Japanese literature; and how fervently devoted his many disciples, friends, and sympathetic critics remain some twenty years after his death. Japanese literature would very possibly still be a closed, parochial kingdom uncharted by outside adventurers without the work that Kawabata did to bring it to the international literary public. Ironic, then, that the greatest gift bestowed by this solitary man to the world of literature was the opportunity to become familiar with a new and compelling body of writing, an encounter of the intimate sort that he never allowed himself in his own life.

* * *

Kawabata Yasunari was born on June 14, 1899, in the city of Osaka. The Kawabata family traced their lineage back almost seven hundred years, to Hōjō Yasutoki, the third military Regent of Japan in the early thirteenth century. Kawabata's father was considered the thirtieth or thirty-first generation from Regent Yasutoki, and such connections elevated the family's status in their local village to the level of dignitaries. Their reputation was further enhanced by the fact that Kawabata family ancestors had built in the village a temple of the Ōbaku sect of Buddhism (a form of Zen which retained a particularly strong Chinese flavor). And though Kawabata's grandfather had not been particularly successful in his management of money or land, Yasunari's father graduated from medical school in Tokyo, began practicing medicine in 1897, and at the time of Yasunari's birth, just two years later, had become assistant director of the Takahashi clinic in Osaka.

Kawabata's father, Eikichi (the name Kawabata uses for the only male member of the traveling troupe of entertainers in "The Izu Dancer"), was thirty years old when his son was born. He and his wife, Gen (born in 1864), had already produced a daughter, Yoshiko, in 1895, but the birth of a first son and heir into this family of status was a cause for great celebration. Eikichi was a sickly, studious man. Eager to continue his studies of medicine and to stay out of the military as Japan entered the Russo-Japanese War, he temporarily changed his name and declared himself an adopted child in order to avoid the draft. His scholarly pursuits embraced not only medicine, but also Confucian learning, Chinese poetry composition, and literati painting. He apparently had a strong interest in literature, for the family library was stocked not only with Chinese books but also with the writings of Chikamatsu, Saikaku, and works of German fiction. His feeble, sensitive nature was passed on to his eldest son, and he shared frail lungs with both his wife and daughter.

What we know of Kawabata's early life is based largely on his "autobiographical fiction." It is often extremely difficult, if not downright impossible, to separate fact from fancy, which leads to speculation. In one story about his youth, Kawabata claimed to have been born two months premature and attributed much of his physical weakness to that fact, but many scholars doubt this.[2] He does, however, convincingly assert that his weak constitution was inherited from his father, that he was unable to eat rice until he entered elementary school, and that the family held out little hope that he would survive to maturity.[3]

Physical infirmity would claim Eikichi's life when his son was only two years old. As he declined from a lung ailment, likely tuberculosis, Eikichi summoned his two young children to his bedside, sat up, and with paper and brush produced two samples of calligraphy which he hoped would provide them with the moral principles to guide them in life after his death. For Yoshiko, then six years old, he wrote the Chinese characters for "chastity." For his weak, two-year-old son, he painted two characters representing "self-protection." Unable of course to grasp the full import of the term, Kawabata interpreted his father's final injunction to mean "stay well."[4]

As though somehow resentfully sensing that much of his life would be spent attending funerals, the young Kawabata behaved erratically at his father's wake. Though he had no memories of the occasion, an aunt later told him, "You absolutely abhorred the sound of the Buddhist gong that they struck at the funeral services. Whenever you heard it, you'd start fretting and crying, so they decided to stop beating it. Then you told them to put out the lights at the altar. And it wasn't enough to extinguish them—you wouldn't be satisfied until they'd broken the candles in half and poured the oil from the lamp cup out into the garden. Your mother wept and was terribly angry...."[5]

After the funeral, Gen took her two children to live with her family in another part of Osaka, but slightly less than a year later, she too succumbed to tuberculosis. The bonds of their family severed, Yoshiko was whisked off to live with her maternal aunt, while Yasunari was taken in by his grandparents. Grandfather Kawabata had managed to lose the family house due to debts, so when he and his wife took charge of their young grandson, they returned to the farming village of Shukunoshō on the outskirts of Osaka, where the family had its origins.

Though it would be wrong to underplay the emotional impact of the loss of his parents on Kawabata, it should be noted that he was treated very warmly, even spoiled, by his grandparents, who must have viewed him as the last slender thread in the family line. Monthly stipends sent from an uncle who was administering the estate of Kawabata's parents kept the three of them comfortable, if not prosperous. Grandfather, who was virtually blind by the time Kawabata moved in with them, was occasionally cantankerous, but at such times Grandmother would intercede on the child's behalf. One such incident is vividly described by Kawabata.

> For some reason I had made my grandfather very angry. That didn't happen very often, but on this occasion he got to his feet and came over to hit me. I ran. It was a simple matter to get away from him, but he came after me nonetheless, bumping into pillars and tearing at the *fusuma* doors (he knew the layout of the house well, but I guess he was flustered and became disoriented). Feeling sorry for the blind old man, I crouched down in a corner of the room. When Grandpa was about to catch me, Grandma stepped in to protect me. In his agitation, my blind Grandfather, not knowing it was Grandma, began to beat her. Backed into a corner of the room, she upset a small cupboard and overturned a teakettle, which got the skirts of her kimono all wet. That was when she finally cried out. Grandpa was astounded and just stood there, Grandma lay on the floor where she had fallen, and I sat huddled in the corner. All three of us burst into tears.[6]

Kawabata began attending elementary school in 1906 along with two other boys and three girls from his village. Like Tanizaki, Kawabata initially protested so adamantly against going to school alone that a neighboring housewife went with him and stayed beside him in the classroom. Eventually he began to meet the other village children in front of the local shrine before going off to school together.

Already at this early period, it seems, a slim barrier had begun to form between Kawabata and his peers. Undoubtedly, the fact that he came from a family with upper-class roots placed him at a distance. But, more important, it was his ill health, his dislike of being around other people, the fact that he lived with his grandparents instead of his parents, and perhaps even the neighborhood gossip that both his parents had died of the dreaded contagion tuberculosis, that stood between

Kawabata and those who should have become his earliest associates. In his writings, Kawabata would later seek to sustain that separation, while at the same time displaying the yearning to be liked by others and to merge into their world free from all differentiation. The longing to melt into "nothingness," to become one with even the objects of nature all around him, is a part of this youthful quest for, and fear of, acceptance.[7]

That initial sense of distance, combined with the realities of his weak physical condition, caused Kawabata to miss sixty-nine days of his first year at school. Some of his absences were the result, no doubt, of illness; others can be attributed to his dislike of school. Another factor was the death that September of his Grandmother, the third death to strike in his immediate vicinity in the space of five years. Though she spoiled him and shielded him from his Grandfather's infrequent fits of anger, Kawabata felt some degree of guilt about the self-indulgent way he behaved toward her. He would later claim that the only day of her life that he showed her any particular kindness was the day she died. The day she took to her bed, neither Kawabata nor Grandfather was particularly surprised, thinking it likely one of her chronic spells of chills or diarrhea. When she muttered to her grandson that she was cold, he placed some socks on her icy feet and covered her with a blanket. "I was so spoiled I couldn't even hold my own chopsticks, and so willful that outsiders were forced to look away when I was around. I had done nothing but make my grandmother cry because I treated her like a slave. This was the first day in my entire life that I had treated her with any kindness."[8] An hour or two later she called out for a neighborhood woman; then, without a final word to Kawabata or her husband, she died.

Only after her death, Kawabata would write, did the Buddhist altar which the family kept in memory of departed relatives come to have tangible significance for him. The only inheritance he had received from his parents, he felt, was a susceptibility to illness and early death. When he learned from a relative that his parents had died of a lung disease, and that he shared their fragile constitution, he began to feel that he was destined to die young, or at the very best to live only to the ages they had attained, and that his sole purpose in life was to wait until the disease could destroy him.[9] Family members would tell him stories about his parents, probably hoping to keep their memory alive, but he promptly forgot every detail, fearing that having their lives fixed in his mind would somehow transfer their disease to him as well.[10]

With the death of his Grandmother, in addition to his own problems, Kawabata missed school more frequently. His performance in the classroom was excellent, however, and his teachers singled him out for his excellent compositions. The villages which sent children to the elementary school competed for the best attendance records, and a tradition of mutual accountability made each child from the village responsible for any other child's absence, so on mornings when Kawabata did not feel inclined to go to school, the half-dozen other children from the village would come to the house to drag him along with them. Fearing this eventuality, his grandfather would close all the shutters, and he and Kawabata would skulk in a corner while the children called out insults and hurled rocks at the shutters. Once it was clear they were going to be late, they flew off to school. Relieved, Kawabata's grandfather would sigh, "It's all right. They're gone."[11]

A fourth family death came at him obliquely. In 1909, his sister Yoshiko, who was fourteen, took ill with a fever (it appears likely that she, too, had contracted tuberculosis), and five days later she died. After their separation seven years earlier, Kawabata had seen her only twice since: in 1906 at Grandmother's funeral, and shortly thereafter when an aunt took him to visit his relatives. Because there had been so little contact over the years, he had almost forgotten that he had a sister, and thus felt no real emotion upon learning of her death. His grandfather, doubtless pained by the loss of another member of his family, urged Kawabata to lament her death, but the boy could only bring himself to taste a kind of pale surrogate of the real grief that his grandfather felt. In later years he would claim to have no recollection of what she looked like. Kawabata was ill on the day of her funeral and did not attend, and for reasons which Kawabata did not disclose, neither did Grandfather. During this school year, his fourth at elementary school, Kawabata was absent a total of fifty-six days. Whether that was connected with his sister's death is not clear.

Living alone with his blind grandfather for the next several years, Kawabata developed some distinctive traits and idiosyncrasies. Perhaps the habit that caused others the most discomfort was the practice he developed of staring into people's faces. He describes this disconcerting habit in an early autobiographical story, "*Hinata*" (A Sunny Place, 1923; trans. 1988).

> I have long had a habit of staring at people who sit beside me. I had often thought to cure myself of this habit, but I found it painful not to look into the faces of those around me. I felt an intense self-hatred every time I realized I was doing it. Maybe this habit came from having spent all my time reading others' faces once I had lost my parents and my home when I was a child and gone to live with others....
>
> After my parents died, I had lived alone with my grandfather for almost ten years in a house in the country. My grandfather was blind. For years he sat in the same room, in the same spot, facing the east with a long charcoal brazier in front of him. Occasionally he would turn his head toward the south, but he never faced the north. Once I became aware of my grandfather's habit of turning to face only one direction, I became terribly concerned. Sometimes I would sit for a long time in front of my grandfather staring into his face, wondering if he would turn to the north even once. But my grandfather would turn his head to the right every five minutes like an electrical doll, looking only toward the south. It gave me a sad feeling. It seemed uncanny. But to the south was a sunny place; I wondered if the south felt ever so slightly lighter even to a blind person.
>
> ... Since he was blind, I often stared fixedly at him. That

had developed into my habit of watching peoples' faces, I
now realized.[12]

The habit apparently remained with Kawabata throughout
his life, no doubt strengthening the impression that he was a
distant, unapproachable man. Mishima Yukio, Kawabata's
brightest literary disciple, related the following in 1956:

> The wretched impression that Mr. Kawabata makes on
> people the first time they meet him is notorious. Because he
> doesn't say a thing but merely stares fixedly at them, those
> the least bit timid are reduced to wiping away beads of cold
> sweat. One young woman, an inexperienced editor, called on
> Mr. Kawabata for the first time. For better or for worse, he
> had no other visitors at the time, but for thirty minutes she
> could not get him to say a word. Unable to bear it any longer,
> she finally burst into tears. Stories of this sort are rife.[13]

Due perhaps in part to his retreat from the world of direct
human interaction, Kawabata became an avid reader. He
claims to have pored over every book in the elementary
school library during his last year there. Adventure stories
were his favorite. He would often climb a tree in his yard, nes-
tle himself in the crotch of the branches, and open a book. He
felt more at ease there than reading in his room.[14] His childhood reading included such all but inaccessible classics as *The
Tale of Genji* and *The Pillow Book of Sei Shōnagon*. Though
he asserts that the meaning of such sophisticated texts was lost
on him, the musical sounds and rhythms of the classical language were imprinted on his mind, and exercised a profound
influence as he began writing himself.[15]

In 1912 Kawabata entered Ibaraki Middle School at the
top of his class. The walk from home to school was almost
three and a half miles, but the continuous exercise helped to
improve his health. By the second year at this school, Kawabata had made a career choice. During his elementary years,
he had dreamed of becoming a painter. He had been particularly good at drawing, and Grandfather had told him stories

about the great Edo painter Kanō Motonobu in the hope of encouraging his grandson. But when Kawabata got to the middle school, he encountered any number of classmates who were better at drawing than he. His incessant reading provided him with an alternative, and he came home one day and announced to his grandfather that he had decided to become a writer. Grandfather gave his approval.

Whether as painter or writer, Kawabata was determined to be a success, if only to restore to the family some of the dignity and property lost in his grandfather's day. Grandfather from his youth had tried his hand at many occupations—growing tea, producing vegetable gelatin—but had failed to attain sufficient income to support his family. As a result, he had been obliged to sell a portion of family lands to a sake brewer.[16] During the family's earlier glory, it had also possessed private burial grounds, separate from the village cemetery, but Grandfather had sold most of that as well, leaving only thirty or forty family gravestones still intact. Kawabata—perhaps more conscious than most of ancestral obligations owing to his frequent attendance at family funerals, and certainly wishing to play a part in fulfilling his grandfather's long-held wish to recoup some of their losses—vowed while in middle school to become rich, buy back the sold cemetery plots, and built a splendid stone fence around the whole as a perpetual defense against future declines in family fortune.[17]

Grandfather did not hesitate to utilize his grandson's budding talents as a writer. The blind man had Kawabata write a letter to his uncle, under Grandfather's signature, bemoaning the meagerness of their monthly stipend. He himself, Grandfather claimed in the letter, was living on nothing but soup, while the poor child was surviving on pickled plums and vegetables—no wonder he was sickly. The letter contained, no doubt, a degree of exaggeration for effect.

Kawabata began writing poetry and brief essays, and assembled them into two collections to which he affixed his late father's *nom de plume*. His verses were all in the new, modern style of the Meiji period made popular by the poetry collections of Shimazaki Tōson, after whom Kawabata modeled much of his own poetry. His earliest known poem, written when he was fourteen, is titled "Reading," and is a spirited defense of the amount of money he spent to buy books; they were, he insisted, purchased because of the "hope" and "sorrow" he bore within his heart.[18] Kawabata wrote his poetry at any time and any place: many verses were composed as he sat, bored, in the classroom. The majority, he confessed, he produced during Japanese-language class.[19]

In the spring of 1914, Grandfather fell ill and took to his bed. Care of the blind, stricken old man fell to Kawabata and a couple of neighborhood housewives. During the last month of Grandfather's life, Kawabata began recording the events of his daily life and his reactions to the loss of his last close relative.[20] In this diary he recounts his grandfather's many frustrated ambitions, describes his dabbling in various kinds of divination—prophecies based upon the configuration of one's face, or even the "physiognomy" of one's house[21]—and details his one success in the home brewing of medicines:

> My grandfather had picked up something of the techniques of Western medicine, and spiced it with his own Chinese pharmacology. He had been dispensing medicine to the country people for a long time. He had an obstinate confidence in his self-taught pharmacology. What strengthened his confidence even more was when there was an outbreak of dysentery in the village.... Some of the dysentery was cured quite readily by my grandfather's medicine.... I do not know how much value it actually had medically, but it was a fact that my grandfather's medicine had shown an uncanny effectiveness.... Then later he ... received permission from the Ministry of Home Affairs to sell three or four kinds of medicine ... but after that his medicine production came to naught.[22]

Kawabata describes his ministrations to the failing body of his grandfather in graphic detail. But what he does not tell us at this time, and in fact does not reveal until 1934, is that he often fled from his grandfather's side during those last weeks, unable to bear the sight of irremediable pain so close at hand, revolted by the old man's helpless inability to relieve himself without aid, and horrified when the old man clawed at his own chest as phlegm caught in his throat. At first he retreated only to the next room to read Tōson's poetry, but eventually he left the house altogether, staying out until after dark, leaving Grandfather to his own devices. When at friends' houses, the later he stayed the more he was gripped by the thought that his grandfather would die utterly alone.[23] Nearly a year after Grandfather died, a female cousin would accuse Kawabata of "heartlessness" for abandoning the old man in his hour of need.[24]

He did, in fact, almost miss the moment of his grand-father's passing, which occurred on May 24, 1914.

> My grandfather died on the evening of the great funeral for the widow of Emperor Meiji.... I am not sure why, but I wanted nervously to attend the national mourning ceremony at school. But would my grandfather die while I was gone?
> Omiyo asked my grandfather about it.
> "It's the responsibility of every Japanese citizen, so go ahead and attend," Omiyo came back and said.
> "Will he still be alive when I get back?"
> "Yes, he will. Go ahead."
> Thinking I might be late for the ceremony, I hurried down the road, but one of the clog straps broke on the way. (At that time we wore Japanese clothing at my school.) I turned around and returned home, dejected at having broken a clog strap, which was commonly held to be a bad omen. Surprisingly, Omiyo said it was just a superstition. She said I should just change clogs and hurry on to the school.
> When the ceremony was over, I was suddenly overcome by a strong feeling of unease. I recall the brightness of the funeral lanterns hung out in front of the houses in town, so it must have been a very dark night. I took off my clogs and ran barefooted all the way home. My grandfather stayed alive until midnight.[25]

Kawabata's behavior at his grandfather's funeral, and again when the family went to collect the cremated bones, suggests that he kept any sense of loss or anguish bottled up inside. He clutched his copy of Tōson's poetry and read from it both on the night Grandfather died and at the wake. On the day of the funeral, while he accepted condolences from assembled friends and family, he suddenly developed a violent nosebleed. Stuffing the corners of his *obi* into his nostrils, he rushed barefoot into the garden and lay on a large rock, waiting for the bleeding to stop. "It was the first nosebleed in my life. It revealed the pain in my heart from my grandfather's death."[26] The nosebleed struck again at the crematorium, and Kawabata had to fling down the ceremonial chopsticks he was using to help collect the bones and hurry off in embarrassment. This time the bleeding refused to stop, and he did not return to the crematorium until he heard voices calling his name nearly a half hour later.[27]

Once his last close relative had been laid to rest, Kawabata was taken into the home of a maternal uncle, and for four months he commuted to school by train. Then, in January of 1915, he moved into the middle school dormitory and remained there until his graduation. Although dormitory life must have had its hardships, there were compensatory pleasures as well. It was in his dorm room, for instance, that Kawabata made his first acquaintance with glass windows. He was so entranced that he moved his bedding near the window so that he could gaze at the moonlight while in bed, but before long he was scolded by a dorm monitor for monopolizing the view. The school had a grass lawn, and he would often stretch out there, or even on a ledge, and read. At other times, he would lie beside the river and write sketches in his notebook of the natural and human scenes that caught his eye.[28] On occasion, whether to amuse his friends or simply to be different, he would amaze his classmates by showing up with his head completely shaven.

Kawabata's range of reading expanded: in addition to the

writings of the Shirakaba-ha (White Birch School), a group of self-affirming young aristocratic writers, Kawabata read Tanizaki's earliest stories, as well as Dostoevsky, Chekhov, and Strindberg. He read Shiga Naoya, but had trouble understanding what he was trying to get at; enjoyed Chikamatsu's plays but had difficulty deciphering Saikaku; and was fondest of all of *Genji*. It did not take him long to fall heavily in debt to a number of bookstores in town.

During his fifth and final year at middle school, in 1916, Kawabata was made a dorm monitor. One of the second-year students in that room, given the pseudonym of "Kiyono" in Kawabata's writing, was a strikingly attractive young man with whom Kawabata embarked upon a homosexual affair. No mention was made of it in any of Kawabata's writings until he serialized an account between 1948–52. There Kawabata would speculate on the reasons he was drawn into the relationship, which he assigned to the unnatural lack of female influence in his home.[29] And yet the affair with "Kiyono," he would claim, "warmed and purified and saved me;" it was, he wrote, his "first love."[30] Never one plagued with an overabundance of self-esteem, Kawabata found an acceptance and an affirmation of himself that he had never felt before, and which he was seldom to experience again.[31]

The time had come for Kawabata to begin publishing his writing. One of his classmates (one whom Kawabata felt had no true literary talent) had submitted a story for publication in a small local newspaper. Spurred by a sense of superior talent, Kawabata showed up one day at the paper's office and asked to meet the literary editor. He announced that he had some works he would like to submit. To his surprise, he was treated with respect, and soon several of his poems, essays, and short fiction were published, his first appearance in print. He also began sending manuscripts off to literary magazines he had been reading for several years; that summer two of his poems were carried.

A mountain of plum blossoms—
A flower-viewing excursion
By wretched village folk.

Early summer rains—
Walking back and forth to the bath,
Transient geishas.

In the fall of that year, the house that Kawabata's grandfather had built in the village was sold to a relation, and with
the proceeds Kawabata not only paid off his grandfather's
debts but also the sizeable bills he himself had accumulated at
local bookshops. A few months later, Kawabata attended the
funeral of his first English teacher (further qualifying him for
the title that a cousin would bestow on him four years later,
"master of funerals"), and joined his classmates in carrying
the teacher's casket to the temple for the Buddhist rites, and
from there to the crematorium. Not long thereafter, he wrote
of the experience in a story, "*Shi no hitsugi o kata ni*" (With
the Professor's Casket on Our Shoulders), which became his
first prose to appear in a magazine.

Two days after graduating from Ibaraki Middle School,
Kawabata left his native Osaka for Tokyo, where he would
live with an aunt and prepare for high school entrance exams.
His grades at the middle school took a downward turn as he
became increasingly involved in literature. As a result, the
school principal and his teachers began to pester him and say
that he was physically and academically unfit, hoping to deter
him from a single-minded preoccupation with writing. Further, they encouraged him to apply to the programs at Keiō or
Waseda, but out of spite he submitted his application to the
First High School, where he was accepted into the English literature department that fall. Another reason for his choice of
First High School was growing pessimism about his own talents as a writer. In the full knowledge that Waseda had produced far more writers in recent years, Kawabata's wavering

confidence led him to opt for the First High School, where he half-desperately hoped that he could at least become a scholar of literature. Surprisingly, his primary reading at high school was Russian literature: he adored Dostoevsky, read *Resurrection* and *The Death of Ivan Ilitch*, but felt no empathy with Tolstoy. He continued the while to dabble in such Japanese writers as Akutagawa Ryūnosuke.

The next three years found him living in the school dormitory. To Kawabata's disappointment, it was run on very different principles from the middle school in Osaka, and eventually earned his antipathy. That, plus his separation from "Kiyono" (Kawabata would attempt to visit his former lover during the summer of 1919, but he was away; their meeting during summer break of 1920 was their last), compounded by uncertainty about his ability to write and a rather desperate state of mind made up of a self-pity and self-hatred that harked back to the "spiritual wounds" received in childhood[32]—all these factors combined to persuade Kawabata that his personality had been unalterably "twisted" as a result of his "orphan's disposition."[33] To clear his head, and perhaps in a quest to find (or, more likely, lose) himself, Kawabata set out for the hot springs resorts of the Izu peninsula in late autumn of 1918. While there, he came across a troupe of performers that he traveled with as far as Shimoda, where Kawabata returned to Tokyo by ship. A couple of early stories deal with the poetry and enchantment of the Izu trip, but he would immortalize the personal experience and the peninsula itself in one of the most widely read and beloved stories in all of modern Japanese literature, "*Izu no odoriko*" (The Izu Dancer, 1926; trans. 1955). The hot springs resorts in Izu became a second home to Kawabata, and for the next decade he spent large parts of each year at a particular hostel at Yugashima.

In fact, Kawabata, like Tanizaki in his college years, became something of a vagabond, moving from one location to another after saying goodbye to the dormitory. Over the course of his peregrinations, he lost virtually all of his keep-

sakes from the past. He had started out with several photographs of his late father, had even displayed one in his room
at his middle-school dorm, but one after another such photos
disappeared like fading memories. By the time he finished
high school, only one photograph of his father and a single
sample of his calligraphy survived (perhaps the death-bed ad-
monition for "self-protection"?). Not a single photograph or
memento of his mother remained. Ultimately, he could no
longer bring himself to think of them as his parents; they were
somehow "neutral" existences, neither relatives nor strangers.[34]

If he was allowing his memories of the distant past to fade,
however, he was taking active measures to retain more recent
experience. Several unsent "love letters" to "Kiyono" he now
boldly turned in as compositions to his high school teachers.
And in 1919 he published an early account of his Izu excursion in the magazine of the First High School literary club. It
was during these high-school days that many of Kawabata's
lifelong literary friends were formed; one, Kon Tōkō, introduced Kawabata to his father, a former sea captain who was
now a devout believer in spiritualism. He inculcated Kawabata with notions of the mystical apprehension of spiritual
things.

One close friend at school happened to frequent a restaurant called the Shirokiya, though what drew him there was
less the cuisine than a beautiful young waitress. He eventually
proposed marriage and was rejected. The young woman in
question appears in Kawabata's early fiction under several
names, most often as "Chiyo." Kawabata, too, was stricken by
her beauty, but was disinclined to compete with his friend.
The friend, however, after a summary rejection from "Chiyo,"
encouraged Kawabata to take up with her. This advice Kawabata was to heed, much to his later sorrow.

As far as frequenting restaurants was concerned, Kawabata maintained that he himself commuted daily between the
Café Paris and the Café Élan in Asakusa for three years run-

ning, rain or shine. He was charmed by the beautiful young actresses who sang cabaret-style songs there, and he would haul some of his friends along to ogle them. One moment that particularly impressed the aspiring writer was the day he caught a glimpse of Tanizaki Jun'ichirō dining at the Nihonkan Restaurant. Someday, he thought, that will be me.

After graduating from First High School in July of 1920, Kawabata moved directly into the department of English literature at Tokyo Imperial University. He rented a private apartment, his first, on the second floor of a hat repair shop in, of course, Asakusa (it was here that he wrote his first critically recognized short story). Not long after Kawabata and some of his old classmates had settled themselves into the university, they began formulating plans to produce a literary journal. As was often the case, they decided to resurrect a journal published by earlier luminaries, hoping perhaps to inherit some of their residual glory. The magazine they decided upon was *Shinshichō* (New Currents of Thought), which Tanizaki and his friends at Tokyo Imperial had worked on a decade earlier. Since the literary figure most recently in charge of the now-defunct *Shinshichō* was Kikuchi Kan, by that time an important power in the literary world, it was deemed vital to obtain his approval before launching the new venture. Kawabata, never hesitant in such matters,[35] promptly marched his band over to Kikuchi's house, introduced the group, and asked for Kikuchi's blessing. A colleague of Kawabata's recalled: "Kikuchi met with us directly, and gave us enthusiastic encouragement, 'Yes, by all means, go ahead and publish it. I'll read it and critique it for you.' We even ended up playing a game of cards with him before we left."[36] Kikuchi, an extraordinarily magnanimous and considerate man (from whom Kawabata would seem to have learned some important lessons in patronage), proved to be one of the most influential benefactors in Kawabata's entire career.

The first issue of the new magazine appeared in February of 1921. A story by Kawabata in the second issue, "*Shōkonsai ikkei*" (A View of the Yasukuni Festival), which centered on a circus troupe, was warmly received by several important critics. Kikuchi, true to his vow, gave the story open critical praise, citing Kawabata's powers of "visualization"; he even gathered the *Shinshichō* coterie together and read the story aloud, punctuating his recitation with frequent exclamations of "This is wonderful, isn't it!"[37] Kikuchi was also instrumental in introducing Kawabata to the man who would become his closest lifelong friend, literary colleague, and benefactor— the writer Yokomitsu Riichi.[38] He further arranged for meetings with some of Kawabata's literary heroes, including Akutagawa Ryūnosuke and Kume Masao. At the end of that year, Kawabata got his first literary criticism published in a major journal and collected his first manuscript fee. Writing clearly took precedence over school studies; during his first year at the university[39] he attended no courses in his major field. Consuming as his writing was, however, his mind was even more consumed by matters of the heart.

By now, at the age of twenty-one, Kawabata had fallen desperately in love with "Chiyo." Even though he was only a college student, had accumulated debts left and right, and could boast only a few yen to his name from his writings, and though she was at this time only fifteen years old, Kawabata was determined to marry. After extracting a promise of marriage, Kawabata rushed to Kikuchi's house to plead for help in placing his translations of English literature. When Kawabata declared that he needed the money because he was planning to marry a young woman, Kikuchi nodded his head vigorously and asked, "So, you're planning to get married, are you?"

Retreating slightly, Kawabata mumbled, "Well, not right away, but—"

"What do you mean? If you've come together, you ought to get married." And without allowing another word of equivocation from Kawabata, Kikuchi opened his heart and his house to the desperate young man. He announced that he was planning to go abroad for a year, and would therefore let Kawabata use his house. Kikuchi would pay a year's rent in advance, and in addition would send an allowance of fifty yen a month to Kawabata. "And I'll ask Akutagawa to recommend your stories to the magazines. That ought to be good enough to help you get through even if I'm not around, don't you think?"[40] Needless to say, Kawabata was dumfounded at Kikuchi's largesse.

That winter Kawabata took a friend and traveled to the "Snow Country" in northern Japan to meet "Chiyo's" father, who worked as a janitor at a village elementary school, to ask for her hand. They sat around a heater in the frigid night-duty room at the school, where Kawabata carefully kept the long sleeves of his shirt pulled down all the way to his palms, so that his prospective father-in-law would not see his spindly arms and worry that he might be surrendering his daughter to an invalid. Before Kawabata could volunteer any information about his background, his friend jumped in and reported that Kawabata's father had died in battle during the Russo-Japanese War. Kawabata blushed, immediately recognizing the motive behind the lie: there was little likelihood that the man would let "Chiyo" marry a feeble-looking creature whose parents had both died of a pulmonary disease.[41]

After all of Kawabata's careful preparations to take a wife, less than a month after they became engaged "Chiyo" sent him a letter telling him that a "catastrophe" had occurred, and that she could not marry him. "The whole thing fell apart so swiftly, so inexplicably," he later wrote. "The experience remained with me for many years thereafter."[42] Kawabata was convinced that she had been enticed by, perhaps even yielded to, another man, but he was never able to find out the exact reason why she broke off the engagement. Throughout the entire ordeal, he insisted upon his own innocence. "Our engagement was verbal," he wrote. "I never laid so much as a finger on the girl."[43] What he sought from the relationship, he wrote in one story, was to be able to return to the "heart of a child" in her presence.[44] There is no reason to doubt the purity of Kawabata's attachment; his closest friend from high school days has written of Kawabata: "If there is anything lacking in him, it is sexual passion, carnality.... From his youthful days he was a man of nature, a man of freedom—so much so, in one sense, that he was not without his licentious side—but still he did not have a whit of sexual passion, sensuality, or carnality in him."[45] The uncanny ability to engage in a sexual relationship without being passionately involved is a model for the kinds of human associations described in works such as *Snow Country* and *House of the Sleeping Beauties*.

The disconsolate Kawabata threw himself into his writing. In February of 1922 he began publishing reviews of contemporary fiction in a widely read monthly, a contribution to critical dialogue that he would continue for the next twenty years. These brief reviews were one of the major channels through which Kawabata expressed his support for new writers, gave his encouragement to authors outside the mainstream, and displayed his catholic aesthetic tastes by granting favorable reviews to writers of every literary camp and school. In April Kawabata transferred from the English literature department to the Japanese literature program. He had managed, through an entire academic year in English literature, to avoid taking a single unit of credit in his major subject. A contemporary has suggested that Kawabata was more fond of soaking in the public bath than of attending classes.[46] Kawabata himself claimed that part of the motivation for the change had to do with an English teacher whose classes were taxing, and the fact that his professors took roll.[47] In any case, the squandered first year of his college career meant that Kawabata would have to spend four, rather than the normal three, years at Tokyo Imperial University.

Kawabata had been receiving monthly living expenses from his parents' estate, forwarded to him by an uncle, until this year at the university. At this point that money dried up, and Kawabata had to begin supporting himself. He became even more actively involved in writing. Over the summer months he sequestered himself at his favorite hot springs resort in Izu (Kawabata would later note that most of his writing had been done "on the road," either while traveling or while staying at an inn or hotel[48]) and wrote a reminiscence of his youthful days, "*Yugashima no omoide*" (Recollections of Yugashima), describing his journey across the Izu peninsula and his affair with "Kiyono." The 107-page manuscript was never published as written, but Kawabata would rework it into "The Izu Dancer" and *Shōnen* (Boys, 1948–52). As a parting gesture to his English literature major, Kawabata also published translations of Galsworthy and Lord Dunsany, as well as a brief Chekhov story.[49]

One of the handful of notable literary journals in twentieth-century Japanese fiction began publication in January of 1923: *Bungei Shunjū*, edited by Kawabata's mentor, Kikuchi Kan. The journal established Kikuchi as the leading force in the literary world, which put Kawabata in a prime position to benefit from his patronage. In fact, by the second issue of the magazine, Kawabata and most of his colleagues who had worked on *Shinshichō* were invited to join the editorial staff at *Bungei Shunjū*, and they gleefully accepted. Kawabata maintained a close relationship with the journal throughout his life, publishing much of his major fiction there, just as Tanizaki was tightly associated with *Chūō Kōron*.

Kawabata's reactions to the Great Kanto Earthquake that September are characteristic. Since his arrival in Tokyo some six years earlier, he had become a fire-chaser, taking advantage of every opportunity to rush out and witness a blazing fire in all its fury. (Kawabata's eagerness to conclude *Snow Country* with a fire scene stayed with him for several years, until he finally added what would become the "last" chapter.) At the time of the quake, he was in his second-floor apartment, but he was uninjured. No sooner had the tremors subsided than Kawabata rounded up his friend Kon Tōkō and scurried over to see Akutagawa Ryūnosuke, whereupon the three promptly began an extended walking tour of the ruins. For two weeks after the catastrophe, Kawabata got up every day, stuffed a jug of water and a tin of biscuits into his knapsack, and wandered the devastated streets of Tokyo until his face was scorched by the sun. His expressionless eyes seemed to take in all the human and physical suffering,[50] but unlike Tanizaki, Kawabata did not view the destruction with any feelings of hope for the rebuilding of a new cosmopolitan capital. Instead, he seems to have felt as if he were attending yet another in a long string of funerals, this one for his city of residence. He was doubtless moved by what he saw, commenting: "No sight of human beings has stirred my heart so much as the endless queues of earthquake victims, looking exactly like refugees."[51] But like the "master of funerals" that he had become,[52] Kawabata had developed the proper degree of ceremonial decorum and allowed no emotion to appear on his face.

Kawabata's undistinguished academic career came to an end in 1924. At the conclusion of his four years at college, he had not accumulated sufficient units in his major to graduate, but his professors took pity on him and allowed him to receive his degree anyway. Particularly solicitous was the renowned literary scholar, Professor Fujimura Tsukuru, who took a measure of pride from the fact that, while his department had given some training to the likes of Tanizaki Jun'ichirō, Shiga Naoya, and Mushanokōji Saneatsu, Kawabata was the first writer to complete the program—after a fashion. Professor Fujimura also encouraged the graduate to apply for teaching positions at two Japanese universities, but Kawabata had no inclination to do so.

The kind of work Kawabata was inclined to do made its appearance that autumn. Along with his good friend Yokomitsu Riichi, Kawabata participated in the establishment of a brand-new literary magazine that was intended as a challenge to all preceding styles of writing and as the hallmark of a new literary age in Japan. Even its name, which had been proposed by Kawabata, suggested something of its editors' audacity,

Bungei Jidai (The Age of the Literary Arts). Kawabata argued that the role which religion had previous played in the lives of the people had now been assumed by literature. Kawabata by his own admission was more actively involved in every phase of the production of *Bungei Jidai* than on any other project of his career.[53] Besides writing critical essays explaining and defending the literary philosophy of the authors appearing in the magazine, he assisted in the editorial work, and even got involved in negotiations with the publishing firm that was to print the journal.

The premiere issue of *Bungei Jidai* came out in October of 1924, and the magazine quickly became a rallying point for writers whose approaches to literature were so modern and so distinctive that they were collectively labeled the Shin-kankaku-ha (The New Perception School), as if they were viewing every incident of the human condition through new eyes. Kawabata himself described how they wished to apply their new perceptions to the writing of literature:

> Our eyes burn with desire to know the unknown. Our mutual greetings are expressions of our delight at being able to discuss together whatever is new. If one man says, "Good morning," and another replies, "Good morning," it is boring. We have become quite weary of literature that is as unchanging as the sun that comes up from the east today exactly as it did yesterday. It is more interesting if one man says, "The baby monkey walks along suspended from its mother's belly," and the other replies, "White herons really have long talons, don't they?"[54]

Inevitably, such a startlingly "fresh" approach to literature is going to have difficulty attracting and retaining followers. While the "Neo-Perceptionist" movement as such lasted a very short time and produced few memorable works, the attempt to adopt some of the techniques of European modernism and the struggle to break away from the flat, overly realistic and autobiographical tendencies that dominated the first two decades of the twentieth century in Japan, are noteworthy achievements. Much that seems surprising, elliptical, and sometimes even odd in Kawabata's writing can be traced back to his days as a Neo-Perceptionist. Casual readers of his fiction may leap to the conclusion that the gaps in logic and development in his stories are techniques derived from his study of classical Japanese literature, but it is rather from the fortuitous blending of a classical consciousness with a modernist technician that such features are born. As Edward Seidensticker has remarked: "Kawabata was well read in avant-garde European literature, with which his fondness for startling images and abrupt transitions has something in common. He was also a student of Japanese literature. His sad themes and frequent ellipses have very ancient origins."[55]

It was in *Bungei Jidai* that Kawabata would publish a number of his "palm-of-the-hand stories," the brief flashes of poetic prose that form a major category in his oeuvre. He remarked, "Most literary men write poetry when they are young; I wrote these vignettes instead."[56] He would produce a great many of these very short works in the 1920s, another batch in the early postwar period, and a final chunk in the 1960s. The total number of palm-of-the-hand stories is 146, and they are often regarded by critics as keys to understanding Kawabata's literature.

As his writing career began to flourish (the "Diary of My Sixteenth Year," describing the days leading to his grandfather's death, appeared in 1925), Kawabata continued to divide his time between Tokyo and the hot springs resort at Yugashima on the Izu peninsula, where his primary preoccupations were playing go and billiards. It was around May of 1925, while he was still in Tokyo, that Kawabata was introduced at the home of a friend to a young woman named Matsubayashi Hideko. Less than a year later they began living together. It seems fairly clear that they regarded their liaison as something like a common-law marriage; they did not bother with the formalities of registering their relationship with public officials until the end of 1931.[57]

In 1926 the Neo-Perceptionist School Motion Picture Federation, headed by the director Kinugasa Teinosuke, was established. Short-lived, it produced only one silent film before being dissolved. But that film, scripted by Kawabata, is regarded by critics as one of the landmarks of experimental impressionist cinema in Japan. Titled "*Kurutta ippeiji*" (A Crazy Page), the scenario is set almost exclusively in an insane asylum, where a man has taken a job as a servant so that he can be near and observe the wife whom he drove to madness. It was named one of the best films of the year and took an award from the All-Kansai Film Association. The filming of *A Crazy Page*, which Kawabata witnessed in Kyoto, is described by film scholars Joseph L. Anderson and Donald Richie.

[Kinugasa] had so little money for his first production, the impressionist *A Crazy Page* ... that his stars—some of them rather big names—had to help paint sets, push the dolly, and make props. He had only eight small lights to work with; so he painted the walls of his small studio silver to make them reflect additional illumination. The picture was shot over a relatively long period, an entire month, and since Kinugasa could not afford accommodations for his actors, they slept on the set or in the front office.... It was shot partly from the point of view of the insane themselves, with impressionistic cutting in the Russian and French avant-garde manner.

... Because of its treatment, *A Crazy Page* was released in theaters specializing in foreign films, but, to everyone's complete surprise, it was at once a big success. At the Shinjuku Musashino-kan it grossed over a thousand dollars a week, which was rather good when one remembers that by this time the admission price of films had fallen to the equivalent of five cents or under. The money was most welcome to the near-bankrupt Kinugasa, who had had to bring the film personally from Kyoto to Tokyo to prevent its being seized by his creditors.[58]

Although the Neo-Perceptionist film group dissolved after the making of *A Crazy Page*, Kawabata's writings would be remade for the silver screen more frequently than perhaps any

of his literary contemporaries. By conservative estimate, nearly thirty films based on Kawabata stories were produced during his lifetime, based on both his serious and his popular
novels.[59] These cinematic treatments certainly helped to boost
public familiarity with Kawabata's writings. Five of those
films were cinematic re-creations of Kawabata's most beloved
story, "The Izu Dancer," which he published in 1926. That
story must be the most frequently filmed in modern Japanese
literature; every time a popular female singer wants to make
the transition into the world of the movies, it seems, "The Izu
Dancer" is the chosen instrument.[60] The role is a marvelous
one for a young actress (except for those past their mid-teens
who, in the key bathhouse scene, must rely on the censor's
bubbles to cover the fact that they, unlike the dancing girl,
have already attained pubescence), but the popular and ideal-
istic view of the story as some kind of youthful initiation into
the world of adult romance is far from the original design.[61]

Like so many of Kawabata works (and, speaking of "The
Izu Dancer," Kawabata once remarked that an author's maid-
en work is his masterpiece), the story would appear on the
surface to be about a young man who tags along with a company of traveling players because of his amorous interest in
the beautiful dancing girl. Our reading of such youthful love-
stories prepares us to find his passions mounting until he discovers that she is still too young—about twelve or thirteen—
for sexual involvement. Thereafter, we presume, he will keep
her at a distance and treat her as a friend, and when the time
for parting comes, it will be bittersweet and tinged with regret,
but not erotic.

But Kawabata thwarts our expectations. While the young
man does initially pursue the girl—literally panting after her
as he ascends the mountain toward Amagi Pass—and while he
does for a fleeting moment fantasize about spending the night
with her, we discover before long that it is not a sexual inter-
lude he seeks at all, but an affirmation of his own worth as a
human being, which he has begun to doubt because of his

twisted "orphan's disposition." He is, to our surprise, filled with joy and relief when he discovers her age, and it is not the realization of a sexual dalliance, but having the girl innocently call him a "good person," that releases him from torment. If this is a love story, it is one played out with the principals at considerable distance from one another, seeking something intensely private rather than any sort of interpersonal involvement.

Although the popularity of "The Izu Dancer" mounted over the years, its publication did not bring Kawabata instant success. He continued to be short of cash even after the story appeared. His first collection of thirty-five palm-of-the-hand stories, titled *Kanjō sōshoku* (Decorations of Sentiment; the case in which the volume was issued bears the romanized title "Décoration de Sentiment"), appeared in 1926, but Kawabata had to sell a copy of it to a used book dealer in order to get train fare to Shinjuku to meet a money lender. For his trouble, the person in question refused to accept a manuscript advance as collateral, a fee promised Kawabata but not yet paid.

In June of 1927, Hideko gave birth to a daughter, who died before she could even be named. Some five years later, Kawabata would write in his "Letters to My Parents" that he feared having a child of his own, and of the enormous responsibility and sadness of bringing into the world a child who might be orphaned as he was. Although he realizes that his wife would make an ideal mother, and that a child of her own would be her one source of hope in her daily life, he cannot induce himself to embark on the "audacious experiment" of parentage. He is more comfortable living with small animals than with children, he writes.[62] Other than this daughter who died at birth, the Kawabatas would have no children.

Kawabata's literary life, however, was moving along well enough. With the help of a senior writer, Kajii Motojirō, who visited him frequently in Yugashima, Kawabata was able to revise the original version of "The Izu Dancer" and publish a story collection with that title. Thanks in large part to Kawabata's presence there, and his enthusiastic recommendations of life on the Izu peninsula, Japanese writers began to flock to Yugashima and its environs for rest and recreation. In April of 1927, however, when Kawabata visited Tokyo to attend Yokomitsu Riichi's wedding, he decided to stay. Summoning his wife, Kawabata would never make his permanent home in Yugashima.

In addition to being one of the most frequently filmed of modern Japanese writers, Kawabata was also one of the most avid participants in the editing of small coterie literary magazines. He mused that he may have belonged to more magazine editorial staffs than any other writer of his day, and he was probably right. Of course, his active participation in the day-to-day business of writing and publishing made Kawabata a variety of friends of various literary persuasions; likewise, his gift for writing impartial reviews, whatever the writer's ideological and or aesthetic stance, owed much to his willingness to lend his name and talents to these small journals. As an "eternal traveler," Kawabata was also a frequent lecturer on literary topics throughout Japan. This, too, would widen the breadth and depth of his reading audience and endear him to many.

In 1929 Kawabata moved near the Asakusa district of Tokyo (this first move within the city was occasioned by his eviction for failing to pay his rent; his second move was to be part of the writers' enclave at Magome[63]), and once again, as in his school days, he frequently strolled through Asakusa Park and spent many of his evenings at the cafés and casinos in the old part of the city. He became a regular at the Casino Folies, the first revue theater in Japan, which opened in July of 1929. Like a French painter frequenting the dance halls of Paris, Kawabata became intimate with many of the club's dancers and artists[64] and took voluminous notes on the life-styles of these demimondes. Those notes he rapidly transformed into a quasi-fictional account of the lively quarter in *Asakusa kurenaidan* (The Asakusa Crimson Gang), which he began serializing in a newspaper that December. The popularity of his descriptive pieces transformed the Casino, theretofore on shaky financial ground, into a busy night spot. Kawabata remarked that he had used only a hundredth of his collected material, and indeed he would later attempt several sequels to *Crimson Gang,* as well as numerous pieces set in the Asakusa entertainment district.

Between 1930 and 1934 Kawabata lectured on literature once a week at the Bunka Gakuin, primarily because his mentor Kikuchi Kan had been named head of the literature department there and insisted that Kawabata come along. Around the same time, Kawabata decided to put into practice his preference for animals over children, and began to raise a small personal menagerie of dogs and birds. At one point he had nine dogs in the house, and late in 1930 he hired a houseboy whose primary responsibility was to walk the dogs. Contemporary accounts suggest that his behavior was, at best, peculiar. Donald Keene notes that "pictures taken of Kawabata at the time show him surrounded by birds, dogs, and other pets, and visitors remembered how, for example, he would casually fling a dead bird into his cupboard."[65] Though he would vehemently deny the connection, Kawabata's behavior during this period of his life seems very much like that of the people-hating, bird-loving protagonist of his 1933 story *"Kinjū"* (Of Birds and Beasts, trans. 1969).

The first love of his life, jilting "Chiyo," paid an unexpected call in March of 1932. Though married, her life had not been a happy one, and she told Kawabata that reading his accounts of their engagement had been a source of comfort and escape. He confessed that he had not been able to keep her out of his mind for five or six years after the relationship had broken up; that he had considered bringing her younger sister to live with them if they had married; and that after she broke off the engagement, he had fantasized about becoming romantically involved with her sister.[66]

In the fall of 1933 Kawabata became one of the editors of

the newly founded journal *Bungakukai*. It was through this medium that he was able to exert some of his greatest influence on the development of modern Japanese literature. Making use of his position there, he introduced the works of such diverse writers as Hōjō Tamio, a young leper who began corresponding with Kawabata in 1934 and who passed away three years later,[67] and Okamoto Kanoko, a woman who wrote to Kawabata asking him to become her tutor in writing. The significance of *Bungakukai* as a literary phenomenon cannot be ignored. Prior to this time, most literary magazines had been associated intimately with specific schools or camps of writing, with their own firm agendas and built-in sets of rivals. Kawabata, as we have already seen, was not comfortable with such a cliquish attitude toward literature, and took advantage of his position as a prominent critic to support whatever individual works he deemed of artistic merit, regardless of their source. Such a stance, manifest in his participation in a wide array of journals, undoubtedly fated Kawabata, as he put it, to "drift with the winds and waters ... hoping always to be able to lose myself, but never completely able to do so,"[68] and was the source of much of the loneliness he felt even while part of a thriving group. But it was a stance that would be adopted by the editors at *Bungakukai*, which was the first journal to be able to bring together writers committed to aesthetic values and those devoted to a proletarian political agenda. Much of the credit for the success of *Bungakukai* must be given to Kawabata.

Kawabata's eagerness to participate in many forms of literary interchange was not always felicitous. In January of 1934 he was persuaded to join a Literary Discussion Group organized by Matsumoto Manabu, who had been head of the Public Security Division of the Home Ministry, one of the governmental organizations involved in censorship. As Donald Keene has noted, "the ultimate purpose of the organization was no doubt to control literature by instituting cooperation between writers and the government."[69] But Kawabata seems to have felt that writers needed to be active participants in such groups, if only to help temper the attitudes of the censors. He would find himself in similar positions during the Second World War.

One other important function which Kawabata served in the literary world was as a member of a number of juries for literary prizes. Many of these prizes were initiated during Kawabata's lifetime, and more often than not he was asked to be on the original selection committee for them: he belonged to nearly as many prize juries as coterie literary magazines. Often these prizes were for new writers, allowing Kawabata to continue his practice of fostering budding talent. Perhaps the most significant prize jury Kawabata belonged to was that for the Akutagawa Prize, an award for new writers instituted in 1935 at the *Bungei Shunjū* by Kikuchi Kan, in honor of his close friend who had committed suicide in 1927. The Akutagawa Prize was then, and continues to be today, the most common route through which a young author is recognized and catapulted into the public arena. Kawabata joined such writers as Tanizaki, Kikuchi, Satō Haruo (still married to Tanizaki's former wife), and Yokomitsu on the original selection jury. The importance of the prize to fledgling authors is amply illustrated by the controversy that arose between Kawabata and a nominee, Dazai Osamu, after the first award was announced.

Dazai, who would gain notoriety for his stories and his outrageous behavior before the war and achieve something like immortality for his novels and suicide after the war, was desperate to win the prize.[70] Learning that he was one of five finalists, he stepped up his self-publicity campaign, focusing his attention on Satō Haruo, whom he knew to be favorably disposed toward his earlier works. What Dazai did not know before the award was announced was that the story he had assumed was nominated, "The Flowers of Buffoonery," was not the work being considered, but rather "Against the Current." Satō, though he liked Dazai's writing, had to admit as the jury met that he considered "Flowers of Buffoonery" a superior work. Kawabata, meanwhile, had thrown his support behind a work by Takami Jun. Three jury members were enthusiastic about a novella by Ishikawa Tatsuzō, and the prize went to him.

In fact, Kawabata had seriously endangered Dazai's chances of winning the prize by writing in his response to "Against the Current" that Dazai's writing "is filled with the author's views on life and literature, but as I see it, there is an unfortunate cloud over his life at present, which regrettably prevents his talent from emerging straightforwardly."[71] Likely Kawabata made reference to the well-known fact that Dazai was a philandering drug addict, but jury evaluations for the prize were published, and in a rage Dazai wrote a public retort to Kawabata that displayed both his frustration and his erratic mentality. After accusing Kawabata of single-handedly selecting Ishikawa as the winner, he made his attack personal.

> Does keeping small birds and watching dancers perform constitute such an admirable life? I thought, "I'll get even. He's a scoundrel through and through." But suddenly I felt, deep in my vitals, the perverse, hot, strong, flannellike affection you have for me. You shake your head. You say I am mistaken. But under the coldness you feign, you warm my body just perceptibly with your fierce, demented, Dostoevskian affection. And you have not the least idea you are doing so.[72]

No one had any idea what Dazai was talking about, though he seems to be attempting to win Kawabata to his side through the power of positive thinking. In a brief published response to Dazai, Kawabata explained in unemotional terms exactly how the jury had made its deliberations. Six months later, when the second prize was to be awarded, Dazai launched a frantic letter-writing campaign, pleading with both Satō and Kawabata to support him. The committee, however, concluded that no work on their short list was worthy of the prize. Dazai resumed his petitions to committee members in June of 1936, hoping against hope to capture the third semi-annual prize. But the jury decided that no author who had previously been nominated could be considered that year. When Dazai found out, he marched straight to Satō's and hurled rocks at the roof of his house.[73] There were clearly limits to the kinds of new writers Kawabata was willing to patronize.

The same month that the first jury for the Akutagawa Prize met to disappoint Dazai Osamu, Kawabata began publishing the stories that would eventually be rewritten and collected under the title *Yukiguni* (Snow Country; trans. 1956). He had, it will be remembered, first traveled to the snowy northern provinces of Japan in 1921, to plead for the hand of "Chiyo." Again in June and the autumn of 1924, he journeyed to the Yuzawa hot springs resort in Niigata prefecture. There he began the writing of his tale of Komako and Shimamura. The way in which *Snow Country* was composed is typical of Kawabata's longer works, and deserves brief mention here. He did not set out with the intention of writing a "novel," as we think of it in the Western sense. Initially he produced a story, "The Mirror of an Evening Scene," which appeared in the January 1935 issue of a magazine. "I didn't write in one continuous breath," he would later explain. "I kept adding to what I had written, as though I had just recalled something, and sent it one piece after another to magazines." The first story "should have exhausted my materials, but I wasn't able to finish the writing by the day of the deadline for *Bungei Shunjū*, so I ended up writing the continuation in *Kaizō*, which had a later deadline that same month. As time passed amidst my absorption with these materials, a remnant of feeling (*yojō*) from them stayed with me, resulting in a work quite different from what I had initially intended."[74]

That "remnant of feeling" would, in fact, remain in Kawabata's head and heart for some thirteen years, until he finally brought the work to "completion." It would later return to harry his mind, exacting from him a palm-of-the-hand distillation of *Snow Country* just three months before his death.[75] One can only speculate about the bonds linking Kawabata and Shimamura; the author admitted that he could not complete the story of Shimamura and the geisha until he had paid several later visits to Yuzawa himself. Though, as with "Birds and Beasts," Kawabata vociferously denied any similarities between himself and the protagonist of *Snow Country*, they are certainly kindred spirits in the way they distance themselves from life. Shimamura's fastidious avoidance of contact with the reality of his career—his refusal to see an actual Western ballet though he is a dance critic, which is "like being in love with someone he had never seen"—is mirrored in the emotional prophylactic he dons in his relationship with Komako, and the detachment is all too familiar in the details from Kawabata's own life. The train tunnel that separates Shimamura's "real" life from his fantasy world in the northern provinces; the misty train window that gives Shimamura a reflected view of Yōko; the "wasted effort" that comes to characterize Komako's life for Shimamura, including her hopeless love for the terminally ill Yukio; the barrier that Shimamura erects between himself and Komako when he calls her a "good woman"—all of these separations, like the mirrors that dominate other Kawabata stories, are part and parcel of the life of disengagement from his surroundings that Kawabata lived himself.

Kawabata's health suffered during the early stages of *Snow Country*, though it is impossible to determine whether the plague of fevers that beset him, resulting in two different stays in the hospital, was the result of his struggles with the story or his conflicts with Dazai. Still, his literary activities continued unabated. When the initial collection of *Snow Country* stories appeared in 1937, Kawabata received a literary prize[76] generous enough to buy himself a summer home in the mountain resort town of Karuizawa. He would spend every summer there until the end of World War II. He took up golf to fortify his health, and became an avid photographer.

Kawabata in his later years.

Kawabata (middle) and literary friends at Ibaraki Middle School.

Kikuchi Kan, Iketani Shinzaburō, Kawabata, and Kataoka Teppei on lecture tour in Tohoku region, 1927.

Kawabata and Yoshikawa Eiji, 1949.

Kawabata at Mishima Yukio's wedding reception, 1958.

Speaking at international PEN conference in Japan, 1957.

Out for morning walk af-
ter learning he had won
Novel Prize, 1968.

Several years later, he would take his camera with him when he scurried over to pay his respects to a friend who had just died, and would snap a photograph of the deceased man's face.[77]

More and more of his time, it would seem, was being devoted to what many might regard as these "wasted efforts," like those of Komako and Shimamura; but these must be considered against the background of social events. By now the militarists had insinuated themselves into the top decision-making groups in the Japanese government, and the invasion of Manchuria was only a few months away. In hindsight, these activities come to seem more like an unconscious effort to disassociate himself from the ugly political realities that he saw all around him than any inability to focus on literature. As an insider in such organizations as the Literature Discussion Group, Kawabata would have been sensitive to the mounting difficulties that official censorship was posing for the Japanese writer, and his retreat into extra-literary activities comes to seem less a mindless diversion than an emotional withdrawal.

One aspect of Kawabata's secession from contemporary society can be seen in the time he devoted, both as an active appreciator and as chronicler, to serializing an account of the *go* matches in which the great master, Honnimbō Shūsai, engaged in the summer of 1938. Kawabata played the part of scribe for newspapers in both Tokyo and Osaka, and the record which he published became so important to him after the death of Shūsai and the conclusion of the war that he revived the material and shaped it into the only one of his works which he considered truly "finished," *Meijin* (The Master of Go, 1942–54; trans. 1972).[78]

Another form of positive retreat, as it were, was his increasing involvement with a program to improve the writing skills of elementary school students. In May of 1939 he helped form the Young People's Literary Discussion Group, where he judged the compositions of over 15,000 students. He also worked with the prestigious writer Shimazaki Tōson

(whose poems he had worshiped as a boy) to edit for publication a collection of the best of these writings. Through these
activities, Kawabata was able to encourage several young
people who went on to become professional writers. At the
same time, he abandoned the writing of monthly reviews,
placing yet another gap between himself and contemporary affairs, and his work with young people became his primary activity during the war years. He would, additionally, increase
the frequency of his travels around Japan, turning more of his
talents toward the writing of fiction for children and popular
audiences.[79]

Kawabata's actions during, and attitudes toward, the war
are somewhat difficult to fathom. On the one hand, he with-
drew personally and professionally from much of the literary
activity that he had displayed in preceding years. Since he
could not count on supporting himself through his curtailed
writing during the war years, he sold his summer house in
Karuizawa and lived off the proceeds. His absorption in *go*
and golf; his commitment to the promotion of youth literature;
his turn to popular fiction and avoidance of propagandistic
writing; and his claim, after the war, that "he had expressed
his rejection of the war ideals and his grief over his fallen
friends in the overtone of his writings"[80]—all of this certainly
suggest a man who was not in sympathy with the motives of
the militarists. He was clearly skeptical of the attempt by the
government to revive popular interest in classical Japanese literature as a means to purge the nation's soul of toxic foreign
elements, but he did turn to the classics again himself, feeling
a need to stake out a definition of what it meant in his own life
to be a Japanese, in the event that his nation and culture were
annihilated in the conflict.

An examination of his wartime activities, however, suggests that in some respects he was willing to cooperate, at
least in minimal terms, with the war effort. He joined the
Japanese Writers' Society, a patriotic group, in October of
1940; undertook three "enlightenment" tours of the Japanese

countryside and occupied territories as part of a move to boost national morale; and was enrolled, as virtually every other author was, in the government-sponsored Japanese Literature Patriotic Association. When the first installments of Tanizaki's *The Makioka Sisters* appeared and the government stepped in to prohibit further serialization of that work, Kawabata essentially supported the censorship when he participated in a roundtable discussion on literature with Shiga Naoya and several other leading writers. Ever eager to smooth over the rough surfaces, Kawabata attempted during the discussion to explain what he saw as Tanizaki's intent in writing so elegantly about the fading bourgeoisie.

> Kawabata: "I wonder if Mr. Tanizaki while he was writing felt attracted by the syrupy, sticky quality of the life he describes, or if he wasn't portraying the stupidity of the bourgeois.... A great many ordinary readers have been fascinated by this book."
>
> Reporter: "Don't you think that young people, even though they may be fascinated, have doubts about its propriety?"
>
> Kawabata: "If the novel causes them to have such doubts, doesn't that prove that it rejects the life it describes? I don't suppose that Mr. Tanizaki, even though he portrays that way of life, intends to encourage it. I am sure that he himself is quite concerned over this."[81]

The slippery undulations of Kawabata's argument may seem ludicrous from our current perspective, but undoubtedly his intention was to effect a satisfactory and amicable solution for all sides of the dispute.

In the late spring of 1941, Kawabata combined a "wasted effort" with an official visit. He was invited by a Japanese newspaper in Manchuria to visit that annexed province. His personal mission was to attend a *go* tournament being held there, but he traveled with an officially sanctioned group and met with several Japanese writers then living in Manchuria. A second visit in September was more formal—he went at the invitation of the occupying Kwantung Army of Japan, and traveled with the president of a major publishing house and the writer/correspondent Hino Ashihei, one of the most active chroniclers of the Japanese military during World War II. Once his official duties were completed, Kawabata parted company and journeyed by himself around various parts of China, collecting examples of folk literature (in 1942 he would edit a collection of folk writings from Manchuria). Kawabata's wife joined him there in October, and they continued their travels. Late in November, when rumors began to circulate of an impending crisis in the war situation in the Pacific, the Kawabatas returned home, just a few days before the bombs fell on Pearl Harbor.

The war years found Kawabata's writing activity circumscribed. The last really typical story he published before the conflict spread across the globe was "*Akusai no tegami*" (Letter from an Evil Wife; later retitled "*Hokuro no tegami*," Letter from a Mole, and translated into English as "The Mole" in 1955). He became involved in yet another new literary magazine, this time primarily because editorial duties allowed him to draw closer to two elder writers whose work he greatly admired—Shimazaki Tōson and Shiga Naoya. He also published several accounts of his childhood, as though the potential for personal and national destruction had forced such memories to resurface. In October of 1942, he obliged the military by paying a required visit to a farming village in Nagano prefecture, where he lectured the peasants on the superior virtues of Japanese literature and culture.

Perhaps his most significant literary pursuit during the war was an act of consecrated editorship. Each December from 1942 to 1944 he sat down and read through pieces of prose and poetry left by those who were setting out to die in battle, and he quoted passages from these works and added his own impressions of them in a series entitled "*Eirei no ibun*" (Posthumous Writings of the Spirits of Fallen Heroes). It was a popular and moving series.

Kawabata undertook one very interesting personal pilgrimage in the spring of 1943. He returned to his ancestral village and there made arrangements to adopt a young female relative, Masako, who was the third daughter of a maternal cousin. Since he (and, one presumes) his wife had decided early on in their marriage that they would have no children of their own, it is fascinating that—with the fate of the nation very much in question—he should determine at this particular juncture in modern Japanese history that the time had come to take an heir.

As the war situation worsened, Kawabata dug an air-raid shelter in his garden, and many times he performed the duties of neighborhood night watchman in his capacity as local chief of fire prevention. His sole consolation during the final two years of the conflict was his reading. He picked up some of the early modern classics—the novels of Natsume Sōseki and Mori Ōgai—and also purchased a copy of Japanese Buddhist texts from a used bookstore. But his primary energies were taken up by a reimmersion in the literature of the classical Heian period. He recollected:

> During the war, after the bombings had become steadily more intense, I took to reading the Kogetsu-shō edition of *The Tale of Genji* in the dimness of nights of blackout controls or amid the miserable-looking passengers on the Yokosuka Line.... As I read I often recalled with what profound feelings the wandering exiles of the Yoshino Court and the people who lived during the wartorn Muromachi period had read *The Tale of Genji*. When I went out on patrol during an alert on nights when autumn or winter moonlight flooded little valleys where not a speck of human-generated light showed, *The Tale of Genji*, which I was then reading, drifted through my mind, and recollections of the people of long ago who had read *The Tale of Genji* in adversity shot through me: I thought that I must go on living, along with these traditions that flowed within me.[82]

Already he had come to think of himself as one of the few

channels through which the flow of Japanese culture could be transmitted into the postwar period.

In perhaps the most personally dispiriting experience he would have during the war, in April of 1945 Kawabata was called upon to visit a naval air base in Kagoshima prefecture, at the southernmost tip of the main Japanese islands. He spent over a month there, associating every day with a group of soldiers who were treated far better than the rank-and-file, served the best meals, and assured a hero's memorial upon completion of their mission: these were the suicide pilots, preparing themselves for certain death.

Just three months before the war ended, in what was perhaps another half-desperate attempt to keep the passageways of cultural communication open at a time when that seemed almost hopelessly clogged, Kawabata solicited donations of books from the personal libraries of important writers in Kamakura,[83] and with them established the Kamakura Bunko lending library. Almost as soon as the war ended, the directors of the library were persuaded to turn their operation into a printing company. The Kamakura Bunko publishing firm undertook two major efforts in an attempt to restore Japanese literature after the war. Kawabata, representing the company, went to call upon some of the deans of Japanese letters, hoping to gain permission to reissue a number of their highly regarded prewar works. His visits took him to see such men as Shiga Naoya and Nagai Kafū. Like Tanizaki, Kawabata seemed to feel he had found a soul-mate in Kafū, perhaps because of the distance the older writer had placed between himself and the military, as well as between himself and contemporary society. Kawabata would visit Kafū half a dozen times in 1946.

At almost the same time they were attempting to revive the popularity of older writers and acquaint postwar readers with some of the finest works of the prewar years, Kamakura Bunko also turned its attention to fostering new writers and providing them with a forum for their work. The magazine they began issuing in January of 1946—one of the earliest

solid efforts to produce a literary magazine after the defeat—
was aptly named *Ningen* (Humanity). No sooner had the magazine begun to appear than a hopeful young writer paid a visit
to Kawabata, eager for patronage. Kawabata was impressed
with the young man's work, and arranged to have the story
"*Tabako*" (Cigarette, trans. 1989) published in the June issue.
The writer was named Mishima Yukio. Though of radically
different literary and political persuasions, Mishima and
Kawabata would remain close until their deaths within two
years of one another.

Kawabata's energies seemed to spurt forth after the war.
He threw himself with full vigor—and perhaps more enthusiasm than he had displayed since the *Bungei Jidai* days—into
his editorial duties at Kamakura Bunko. He faithfully commuted to the firm's office in Nihonbashi every day and remained active in his editing duties there until it went bankrupt
in 1950. He published a story in the first issue of *Ningen* and
produced a new chapter for *Snow Country* in May of 1946.
With other leading writers he helped start a literary magazine
for children. He moved to the Hase area of Kamakura, where
he would remain for the rest of his life.

Yet some of the flurried activity seems almost a mask for
an underlying pain. Kawabata, most surely, was deeply hurt
by the defeat of the nation he loved. After claiming that he
had suffered no direct personal loss or inconvenience because
of the war and defeat, Kawabata went on to say:

> I have always grieved for the Japanese with my own
> grief; that is all. As a result of the defeat, that grief must have
> permeated my flesh and bones. But the defeat actually
> brought freedom of the spirit and the sense of what it means
> to live in peace.
>
> I consider that my life after the war consists of "remain-
> ing years" and that these remaining years are not mine but a
> manifestation of the tradition of beauty in Japan.[84]

Elsewhere he would remark, tellingly, that there was nothing left for him now but to return to the ancient mountains and rivers, return to the sorrows inherent in Japan's past, and produce only elegies for the lost Japan. As one Japanese critic has observed, in the postwar period Kawabata "sensed within the defeated people of Japan the same orphaned condition that had been his own in the past."[85]

Such sorrow was brought home to Kawabata and personalized for him as one after another his closest friends in the literary world died in a short space of time following the defeat, and once again Kawabata had to assume the role of "master of funerals." It was a role he now undertook with dignity, stepping forward from the crowd of mourners to read the eulogies of fallen friends—the writers Shimaki Kensaku, Takeda Rintarō, Hayashi Fumiko, and Hori Tatsuo; his dearest friend Yokomitsu Riichi; his erstwhile mentor Kikuchi Kan—leading the reading public in mourning.[86]

Between assignments at the publishing office and funerals, Kawabata began to take an active interest in classical art, and he now visited art galleries and exhibits with the same enthusiasm that he had once frequented cafés and dance halls. He acquired a substantial collection of art work himself, specializing in eighteenth-century paintings as well as contemporary works by both Japanese and Western artists.[87]

Snow Country, in the form it is known to Western readers, was "completed" in 1947—though Kawabata would insist that it was still not good the way it ended, but that he had no idea how to finish it.[88] Shortly thereafter, the Shinchōsha publishing company began to issue a sixteen-volume collected works, and Kawabata expended considerable energy rounding up old diaries and letters, original manuscripts of well-known works, and producing lengthy personal commentaries for each volume. It was one of the few times in his career that he was open and voluble about himself.

And then came the PEN Club. The international association for poets, essayists, and novelists had first established a chapter in Japan in 1935, with Shimazaki Tōson as its president.[89] Kawabata attended the meetings in February of 1947 that would lead to a postwar reestablishment of the society. Then, with the resignation of Shiga Naoya as president (echoing, certainly, his feeling that he was very much a prewar writer), Kawabata was elected fourth president of the Japan PEN Club on June 23, 1948. He would hold the position for almost two decades, during which time he would again throw himself into activity that was anything but "wasted effort." His paramount achievement as PEN president came with the international writers' conference he organized in Tokyo in 1957, which will be described below.

Stops and starts characterized Kawabata's early postwar literary production. Throughout 1948, he serialized a translation into modern Japanese of a Heian classic, the *Torikaebaya monogatari* (trans. as The Changelings), but he was unable to complete it. He also intended to produce his own modern-language version of *The Tale of Genji*, as Tanizaki had done, but that project never got under way. He hoped to write a novel about the bombings of Hiroshima and Nagasaki but never achieved that goal. Before he finally hit his stride in 1949, he turned once again—and, essentially, for the last time—to his youth for materials to shape *Shōnen* (Boys, 1948–52), describing his encounter with the Izu dancer and his affair with "Kiyono."

The cool, distant eyes which Kawabata cast upon all events around him continued to haunt and sometimes irritate his contemporaries. In November of 1948 he was commissioned by the *Yomiuri* newspaper company to attend a session of the Tokyo War Crimes trials and report his experience. Exactly a year later, the city of Hiroshima invited Kawabata along with other PEN members to view the devastation wrought by the atomic bomb. Again in 1950, he would travel with PEN writers to Hiroshima and Nagasaki to examine the human and physical damage. After each visit to the bomb sites, as if he needed tangible affirmation that something of Japan had survived the horrid war, Kawabata detoured to

Kyoto, where perhaps the ancient temples and gardens helped restore some sense of spiritual equilibrium. Kawabata was criticized for "trivializing" the significance of the nuclear destruction by capering in the old capital immediately after his visits to Hiroshima and Nagasaki, but such critics no doubt expected the kind of open, outward response from Kawabata that he could not deliver. That he was moved by what he saw in the ruined cities is beyond question; he used his position as PEN president to make many public pronouncements in support of world peace and disarmament, including a declaration for peace (later published under the title "Weapons Invite War") at the PEN-sponsored conference "World Peace and Literature" held in Hiroshima in 1950.

An especially productive period began for Kawabata in mid-1949. He published the first segment of *Senbazuru* (A Thousand Cranes; completed 1952; trans. 1959), and four months later the initial installment of *Yama no oto* (Sound of the Mountain; completed 1954, trans. 1970). Neither of those works was finished before he began the serialized publication of *Maihime* (The Dancing Girl, 1950–51). The publication histories of both *A Thousand Cranes* and *Sound of the Mountain* resemble the erratic, scattered pattern Kawabata set with *Snow Country*, though they do not stretch over as long a period of time or undergo as many major revisions. But the technique of evolving narration—with one segment suggesting, through the "remnant of feeling" that lingered within Kawabata's mind, how yet another moment in the lives of his characters could follow that which preceded—had become a key pattern for Kawabata's writing. The comparison that has frequently been made between Kawabata's method of storytelling and the medieval art of linked verse (*renga*) is entirely apt. His sense of narration little resembles what Western readers normally regard as "plot development," since his stories often lack a story line and seldom develop. A sense of the meanings of time and action and individual volition which is very different from that of the West is clearly in operation in a

Kawabata "novel," suggesting that they should not be called novels at all, but rather, perhaps, linked prose.

The essentially fluid nature of Kawabata's fiction made it possible for him to say that many of his works could end at any point, and that specific chapters could easily be deleted. Perhaps in no instance, however, was the truly ephemeral quality of his writing more evident than with a volume published in 1952 (so highly esteemed that it was given a literary prize by the Japan Art Academy), which included all of the sections of *A Thousand Cranes*, as well as the parts of *Sound of the Mountain* that had already appeared, implying that two completely unrelated narratives—one finished, the other in progress—could be brought together into as coherent a volume as the tenuously related stories that would eventually find their place on bookstore shelves as two separate "novels." Only a month after that volume appeared in hardback, Kawabata published a new segment of *Sound of the Mountain*. That novel was made into a movie even before Kawabata had finished writing it. An intended sequel for *A Thousand Cranes* was commenced in 1953, but while he was traveling in Kyushu he lost an entire briefcase stuffed with notes for the new work, dashing his hopes of completing it.

In 1953 Kawabata was elected a member of the Japan Art Academy, along with Nagai Kafū. He continued to be active on literary prize juries, once again becoming a juror on the Akutagawa Prize committee when that award was revived in 1949, and exerted his influence over literature as he had done in prewar years. 1954 saw the completion of *Sound of the Mountain* and *The Master of Go*. If Kawabata's early writings are best represented by "The Izu Dancer," in which the distance between characters takes the form of the gulf separating the shy student from the beautiful but immature dancer; and if mid-career works such as *Snow Country* display an emotional breach opening between a man unwilling to commit himself and a woman who cannot live without such a bond; then in late works such as *Sound of the Mountain*, the alienation of one human being from another is represented in a rich variety of ways.

Shingo realizes even as the novel opens that he is no longer a distant observer of the phenomenon of death, but that it rumbles within his own ears, warning him that he draws daily closer to its borders, and that the deaths of many of his closest friends are merely reminders of his own finitude. As he approaches the ultimate separation from life, he finds himself being severed from virtually every aspect of daily experience: he can no longer tie his tie; he cannot remember the name of the maid who recently left their employ; he feels no warmth toward his own wife and children; even his own head he would like to remove and send out to the dry cleaners. He walks through life as though enveloped in a bubble, able to see what goes on around him but increasingly unwilling to play a role. That for which he most eagerly yearns—the affection of his daughter-in-law, Kikuko, and, even more remotely, the woman far off in the past who died before he could marry her, leaving him to settle for marriage with her sister—is beyond his reach. These relationships, because they are at the most impracticable, most impossible distance from him, become the ones he cherishes most. The single act of enthusiasm he displays in the novel comes at the end when he decides to revisit the place where he met and fell in love with his then untouchable and now dead sister-in-law.

The story of *The Sound of the Mountain* is, then, fundamentally about the process through which a man at the portals of death severs his ties with the realities of his daily existence and prepares for the step into the void. This raises the intriguing question of Kawabata's characterization of his postwar works as "elegies." The distances which Shingo, the protagonist, begins to create between himself and the people and events around him come to seem more than just a personal act of preparation for the grave. The depictions of contemporary life—with his son Shūichi's infidelities, the twin abortions of Shūichi's wife and mistress (whose names are almost homophonous), and the litter of useless children which his daughter Fusako keeps parading through the house—are almost uniformly distasteful. Thus it seems evident that Shingo—and Kawabata—are separating themselves from more than just the details of a single individual's life. *The Sound of the Mountain* can be read almost as a rejection of the very notion of life in postwar Japan, where every relationship is one of deception and disappointment, where every attempt to reproduce is aborted or futile, and where the loss of all sources of beauty—whether the remembered beauty of the dead sister-in-law or the beauties of profuse nature which only Shingo and Kikuko seem to notice—marks the end of any kind of life that could be regarded as worth living. Kawabata in this novel separates himself from all that is modern and contemporary, and leaves us with nothing but a despairing realization that our memories of the past, and of traditional beauty, will sustain us only until we take the final step into the grave. The novel has been described by one major critic as "not only Kawabata's masterpiece, but ... the very summit of postwar Japanese literature."[90]

With his finest postwar novel behind him, Kawabata spent the next several years writing in different media, with mixed success. He became addicted to sleeping pills around 1954, which would have a deleterious effect on his writing. He produced several middlebrow novels, serialized in newspapers and women's magazines.[91] He also wrote two scripts for dance-dramas that were performed both by the Nishikawa school of Nagoya dance and by the popular Takarazuka musical theater troupe. He remained active in PEN Club activities, sending official messages of greeting to international PEN conferences and telegrams of support to the Hungarian people at the time of their anti-communist revolt in 1956.

It was, in a very real sense, because of Kawabata that the linguistic and cultural barriers which had isolated modern Japanese literature from the rest of the world were finally toppled, and Japanese writers were able to take their place alongside their contemporaries on the international literary scene. Kawabata's writings were some of the first to be translated into English and several European languages in the mid-fifties and to gain both popular and serious critical attention. Edward Seidensticker's abbreviated translation of "The Izu Dancer," a fitting introduction to Kawabata for Western readers, appeared in *The Atlantic Monthly* in 1955, and the following year he rendered *Snow Country* into English. These were sufficient to whet the appetites of readers interested in both the exotic and the familiar in modern-day Japan, and with the enthusiastic cooperation of an enlightened editor at a major US publisher, more translations from the Japanese were undertaken.

If the translation of Kawabata works first brought popular attention to modern Japanese fiction, the twenty-ninth international PEN conference, convened in Tokyo and recessed in Kyoto in September of 1957, earned it respectability. Kawabata spared no energy or effort in planning and publicizing the gathering. He traveled to the PEN executive committee meeting in Europe to set the initial plans for the conference; while there, he met with such authors as Francois Mauriac and T. S. Eliot. After the executive meeting, Kawabata paid courtesy calls to France, England, West Germany, Italy, Denmark, and several Asian countries to extend official invitations to the Tokyo conference. His overseas excursions on behalf of Japan PEN, and, indeed, on behalf of all contemporary Japanese writers, consumed almost two months. The conference was an enormous success, on a par with the Tokyo Olympics of 1964 in the respect it would bring to the nation, attracting many writers and critics from across the globe, along with every leading literary Japanologist of the day. The felicitous meeting of writers and Japan hands, carefully orchestrated by Kawabata, inspired translators to undertake more renditions from Japanese, and encouraged non-specialists to seek out the Japanese works being made available one after another. Scurrying about behind the scenes, performing the miraculous feat of bringing disparate camps together for communication, was the familiar figure of Kawabata, who had been effecting such fusions of dissimilar minds since his days as a literary critic, when, from his distant position of strict neutrality, he had been able to bring proletarian and art-for-art's-sake writers together in the same book review or journal publication.

Kawabata's tireless efforts in organizing the PEN conference did not go unrecognized. Donald Keene in his landmark *Modern Japanese Literature: An Anthology* acknowledged the role Kawabata had played as go-between for authors and translators; the Association for the Promotion of Japanese Literature awarded him the Kikuchi Kan Prize (an honor he must surely have appreciated in light of all Kikuchi had done for him as a fledgling writer); the international PEN Club, impressed by his abilities as both a writer and an organizational leader, designated him an international vice president; at the PEN conference in Frankfurt the following year, he was awarded the Goethe Medal, both for his efforts in coordinating the convention and for the high critical esteem received by European translations of *Snow Country* and *A Thousand Cranes*; he visited the United States at the invitation of the State Department in May of 1960; he received a cultural decoration from the French government; and in 1966, the Japan PEN Club, still grateful for all he had done on their behalf, presented Kawabata with a commemorative bust of himself which had been sculpted by Takada Hiroatsu. The highest international award, however, was still a few years away.

The unflagging promotion of the work of others, however, is bound to take its toll on an individual's literary output. His service on behalf of Japan PEN, combined with a painful gallstone attack that hospitalized him from the summer of 1958 until April of the next year, drastically reduced Kawabata's own literary production. In 1959, in fact, he published no new fiction, his first unproductive year since his career began. This stalling of his creative engines would not last long, however: in January of 1960 Kawabata began serialization of one of his last great works, *Nemureru bijo* (The House of the Sleeping

Beauties; completed 1961, trans. 1969). This work powerfully suggests that the advent of old age (Kawabata was sixty-one) brings with it yet another agonizing form of isolation: the loss of the physical powers of sexual intercourse without the loss of the emotional desire for intimate contact. *Sleeping Beauties* is a bleak portrait of the little that is left for those who have never been good at forming relationships; it is matched in its pessimism only by a later story, "*Kataude*" (One Arm, 1963–64; trans. 1967), in which a woman has so become an "object" in the eyes of her lover that, with equanimity, he can remove her arm and take it home with him.

That final creative surge—in which some would include the 1961–62 novel *Koto* (The Old Capital; trans. 1987) but usually not *Utsukushisa to kanashimi to* (Beauty and Sadness, 1961–63; trans. 1975)—would earn Kawabata the highest cultural award bestowed by the Japanese government, the Medal of Culture (*Bunka kunshō*), in November of 1961. But his life and his writings were coming open at the seams. His addiction to sleeping pills reached a peak during the composition of *The Old Capital*, and when he finally made the decision, shortly after that novel was completed, to give them up, he fell into a coma and lay unconscious in the hospital for a full ten days. For some time he would continue to fight the addiction's after-effects. Though he would begin several other works, the bulk remained unfinished, and the final contributions of his life to the world of Japanese literature would be largely institutional or ceremonial, not creative.

One of his last important achievements was his role in the establishment of a library and museum devoted to the promotion of modern Japanese literature, the Nihon Kindai Bungakukan (Museum of Modern Japanese Literature) in Tokyo. He was directly involved in planning for the museum, nurtured it through to its completion in 1967, served it as honorary advisor and member of the fund-raising committee, and was named honorary director shortly before his death. He continued to attend PEN conferences in Saõ Paolo and Oslo as an international vice president, but resigned his position as president of the Japan PEN Club in October of 1965, after seventeen years of distinguished service. He continued as funeral master for literary colleagues, reading eulogies for Ozaki Shirō and Satō Haruo in 1964, Tanizaki in 1965, and Mishima in 1971. Kawabata was in attendance when his maiden work was officially canonized: in November of 1965, a commemorative statue depicting a young dancing girl and a First High School student was unveiled at the Yugano hot springs in Izu. (Four years later, his alma mater, Ibaraki Middle School, would erect a literary monument in his honor.)

Early in 1966, Kawabata was hospitalized for three months with a liver disorder. Two years later, when his friend from school days, the writer Kon Tōkō, ran in the elections for the Japanese Diet, Kawabata became actively involved, serving as campaign chairman and speaking into a blaring loudspeaker on streetcorners in the kind of popular electioneering that is typical of Japanese politics. Then, in October of 1968, Kawabata was notified that he had been selected as the first Japanese writer to receive the Nobel Prize in Literature. With the characteristic generosity that had graced his public life for decades, Kawabata invited his chief translator, Edward Seidensticker, to accompany him to the ceremonies in Stockholm and to translate his acceptance speech, "Japan, the Beautiful, and Myself"[92] before the Swedish Academy in December. The speech is a curious hodgepodge of quotations from classical Japanese poets and priests, blended with some interesting aesthetic observations by Kawabata. Citing a Japanese scholar of Botticelli, Dr. Yashiro Yukio, Kawabata states:

> One of the special characteristics of Japanese art can be summed up in a single poetic sentence: "The time of the snows, of the moon, of the blossoms—then more than ever we think of our comrades." When we see the beauty of the snow, when we see the beauty of the full moon, when we see the beauty of the cherries in bloom, when in short we brush against and are awakened by the beauty of the four seasons, it

is then that we think most of those close to us, and want them to share the pleasure.... The snow, the moon, the blossoms, words expressive of the seasons as they move one into another, include in the Japanese tradition the beauty of mountains and rivers and grasses and trees, of all the myriad manifestations of nature, of human feelings as well.[93]

Kawabata basked in Japanese and international acclaim for the next four years. The Japanese Diet officially congratulated him; along with Alexander Solzhenitsyn and Stephen Spender, he was elected an honorary member of the American Academy and Institute of Arts and Letters, as Tanizaki had been in 1964; he was invited to lecture at the University of Hawaii in the spring of 1969, and received an honorary doctoral degree there and at Hanyang University in Seoul; later that same year the Japanese consulate in London sponsored a Kawabata Yasunari exhibit; as special cultural emissary he attended and lectured at the Japan Week celebration in San Francisco, commemorating a century of Japanese immigration in 1969; an Association for the Study of Kawabata Literature was inaugurated in 1970; and that year, a fifth edition of his collected works was published.

Through it all, however, he was publishing no new fiction. The sudden celebrity that attended the Nobel Prize, the debilitating flurry of public scrutiny, has often been cited as a major factor in Kawabata's emotional and physical deterioration. A deep personal wound came with Mishima's *seppuku* in November of 1970. Kawabata was, in fact, just leaving the funeral of another friend when news of Mishima's disembowelment reached him. He rushed to the Self-Defense headquarters, but was not allowed to see the body because the police inquiry had already begun. In an article about Mishima's death published two months later, Kawabata concluded by saying: "With regard to Mishima's act of death, at the present time I wish to say nothing."[94] But in a letter written to Harold Strauss at the Knopf publishing house in New York just thirteen days before Kawabata's own death, he appended a postscript which read: "There is not a single moment when I am free of the grief and sorrow I feel over Mishima's lamentable death."[95]

Although he would rally himself a few months after the incident and once again campaign for a friend who was running for mayor of Tokyo, and would further damage his weakening constitution with attempts to raise funds for the International Conference on Japanese Studies (which attracted 199 Japanologists from 39 countries), these now seem almost desperate attempts to rouse his enthusiasm for life. In his final months, he gave a lecture titled "I Wish I Could be a Newcomer," spent a week in the hospital with appendicitis, and published an essay called "Dreams Are Like Phantoms."

At around six P.M. on April 16, 1972, Kawabata went to an apartment at Hayama that he had been using for several months as his workplace. He was found there, dead from gas inhalation, with no suicide note. Those closest to him still vehemently argue that his death was surely accidental.[96] Others, allowing him a margin of doubt, suggest that death by his own hand was less an act of volition than the ultimate separation from life that had been his lifelong literary theme. The funeral services were cosponsored by the Japan PEN Club, the Japan Writers Association, and the Museum of Modern Japanese Literature, organizations he had served faithfully and with extraordinary success. Into his casket were laid his favorite fountain pen, a hundred sheets of blank manuscript paper, his pipe and glasses, a volume of his selected writings, a crested kimono, and the purple ceremonial *hakama* he wore when he accepted the Nobel Prize. Roughly interpreted, the posthumous Buddhist name given him by his friend Kon Tōkō means, appropriately enough, "a mirror of literature on a solitary mountain." National exhibitions in his honor toured Japan for eight months, a Kawabata Yasunari Memorial Society was founded with Inoue Yasushi as president,[97] and the Museum of Modern Japanese Literature named a reading room in his honor.

It takes some mental adjustment to reconcile the two divergent portraits of Kawabata that emerge from an examination of his life. The public Kawabata always seemed to be on the run, scurrying about on behalf of some undertaking larger than just himself, attempting to reconcile the differences between opponents across the literary spectrum. The portrait of *that* Kawabata is of a magnanimous mediator, a go-between who put the interests of others ahead of himself. Not only did he labor to smooth out the conflicts between writers of rival camps, he also, as a master of funerals, did all within his power to ease the way of those whose souls had just departed this life.

The other Kawabata that emerges from a study of his life is a man who was infinitely discomfited by human contact. Here is the orphan, the jilted lover, the student roaming Izu, the lover commuting to the *Snow Country*, the aged patriarch discovering that his strongest yearnings are for those who are forever denied him. The temptation is strong to imagine that, like the student in "The Izu Dancer" who found acceptance (but not love) among vagabond entertainers, Kawabata himself would have been pleased to discover that the warm tears which flowed from his eyes were clearing his head of all thought and emotion, leaving him with only a pleasant, empty feeling. That, like Shimamura, Kawabata found the most alluring beauty within the dark tunnels that separated him from the vibrancy of human contact. And that, just as Shingo in *Sound of the Mountain* allowed his heart and mind to be drawn with mounting intensity into the irretrievable past, Kawabata also took his greatest comfort from the literature of past eras, the loves that had been lost to him in his youth, and the memories of friends and family who had repeatedly deserted him through death.

And so, although every Kawabata work is set in the modern period; and though in literary technique he is as much a Western-style modernist as he is a Japanese-style antiquarian; and though in very real terms he contributed more than perhaps any other individual to the legitimization of contemporary Japanese fiction in the international world—in spite of all this, Kawabata seems not to belong to the society in which he lived. Abandoned—though not from spite—as a child, spurned as a young lover, wary of others (and himself) as a fledgling writer, and perpetually dressed in the clothes of mourning in the postwar world, it comes to seem only natural that Kawabata's characters should find themselves alienated from the people around them. He could only speak the truth to another person, Kawabata once wrote, when it was to their back.[98] None of his characters truly grapple with the urge to reject modernity in favor of the past, as do some of Sōseki's or Tanizaki's protagonists. They seem rather to exist in the void, too uncomfortable to make a place for themselves in the present day, but too conscious of the fact that there is no longer a past to return to. Perhaps that is the difference between a Meiji writer like Sōseki, who still lived amid relics of the past, and Kawabata, for whom such relics had been forever destroyed or degraded; and, again, the difference between Tanizaki, largely a Taishō writer in spirit who was able to imagine a past of his own within the shadows of childhood memory, and Kawabata, the thoroughly Shōwa writer, who, like his emperor, unconditionally surrendered all concrete claims to the past. At the conclusion of such a life, death— whether consciously selected or not—seems less like an unwelcome visitor than a natural step in Kawabata's move away from contact with the world.

NOTES

Natsume Sōseki

1. Edwin McClellan, *Two Japanese Novelists: Sōseki and Tōson* (Tokyo: Charles E. Tuttle, 1971), p. 3

2. Trans. by Edwin McClellan, in his introduction to *Grass on the Wayside* (Tokyo: Charles E. Tuttle, 1971), pp. vii–viiii; original quotation in the first *Sōseki zenshū*, 20 vols. (Tokyo: Sōseki Zenshū Kankōkai, 1928), 13:416–18

3. *And Then*, trans. by Norma Moore Field (New York: B. G. Putnam's Sons, 1982), p. 72

4. Discussed by McClellan in *Two Japanese Novelists*; original information in the 1928 *Sōseki zenshū*, 20:507–8

5. Donald Keene, *Dawn to the West* (New York: Holt, Rinehart and Winston, 1984), p. 307

6. Jay Rubin, trans. , "*Watakushi no kojinshugi*," *Monumenta Nipponica* XXXIV, 1 (Spring 1979), p. 32

7. From the second *Sōseki zenshū*, 17 vols. (Tokyo: Iwanami Shoten, 1967), 12:344

8. Ibid., 12:353

9. McClellan, *Two Japanese Novelists*, p. 7

10. 1967 *Zenshū*, 12:378–9

11. Ibid., 12:186

12. Quoted, with slight modification, from *Kodansha Encyclopedia of Japan* (Tokyo: Kōdansha, 1983), 5:350

13. McClellan, *Two Japanese Novelists*, p. 7

14. Rubin, trans., "*Kojinshugi*," pp. 31–2

15. McClellan, *Two Japanese Novelists*, p. 8

16. Toshiaki Tsukamoto, "Sōseki, His Scholar-Critic Years (1890–1909)," in Takehisa Iijima and James M. Vardaman, Jr., eds., *The World of Natsume Sōseki* (Tokyo: Kinseido Ltd., 1987), p. 24

17. McClellan, *Two Japanese Novelists*, p. 9

18. Ibid.

19. Ibid.

20. Etō Jun, *Sōseki to sono jidai*, 2 vols. (Tokyo: Shinchōsha, Shinchō Sensho, 1970), 2:15–19

21. Ibid., p. 21

22. From Kyōko's memoirs; cited by Etō in *Sōseki to sono jidai*, 2:33–8

23. Rubin, trans., *"Kojinshugi,"* pp. 31–2

24. Etō, *Sōseki to sono jidai*, 2:47–8

25. Ibid., p. 42

26. Keene, *Dawn to the West*, p. 349, n. 2

27. 1967 *Zenshū*, 13:28

28. Ibid., 13:23–24

29. Ibid., 13:26–27

30. 1967 *Zenshū*, 13:24–5

31. Ibid., 13:17

32. Ibid., 13:18

33. McClellan, *Two Japanese Novelists*, p. 11

34. Etō, *Sōseki to sono jidai*, 2:84

35. 1967 *Zenshū*, 13:76

36. Ibid., 13:34

37. Ibid., 13:37

38. See Keene, *Dawn to the West*, p. 311; Norma Moore Field, Afterword to her translation of *And Then*, p. 262; and McClellan, *Two Japanese Novelists*, p. 11

39. 1967 *Zenshū*, 13:54

40. Ibid., 13:36

41. Etō, *Sōseki to sono jidai*, 2:86–7

42. 1967 *Zenshū*, 13:40

43. Ibid., 13:34

44. Ōgai was one of those enviable renaissance men, combining a highly successful literary career—second only to that of Sōseki's in prewar Japanese literature—with a full-time career as a doctor for the Japanese army.

45. Ibid., 13:42–3

46. Ibid., 13:57. In fairness to Sōseki, it should be noted that his personal copy of the Bible, preserved in the library at Tōhoku University, is filled with marginal notations written in Sōseki's own hand. See Kii Nakano, "Christian Milieu and Sōseki's *Sanshirō* and *Mon*," in *The World of Natsume Sōseki*, p. 174

47. Rubin, trans., *"Kojinshugi,"* pp. 33–5

48. 1967 *Zenshū*, 13:70

49. Tsukamoto, "His Scholar-Critic Years," p. 29

50. Quoted in the Translators' Afterword in Sōseki's *To the Spring Equinox and Beyond* (Tokyo: Charles E. Tuttle, 1985), pp. 319–20; trans. by Kingo Ochiai and Sanford Goldstein

51. Quoted by Jay Rubin in the Afterword to his translation of Sōseki's *The Miner* (Stanford: Stanford University Press, 1988), p. 165

52. Keene, *Dawn to the West*, p. 320

53. Ochiai and Goldstein, Translators' Afterword in *To the Spring Equinox and Beyond*, p. 324

54. See McClellan, *Two Japanese Novelists*, p. 15

55. See Keene, *Dawn to the West*, p. 333

56. Keene, *Dawn to the West*, p. 342

57. Rubin, trans., *"Kojinshugi,"* pp. 40–42

58. Trans. by Maria Flutcsh, from her article, "An Introduction to Sōseki's Chinese Poetry," in *The World of Natsume Sōseki*, p. 12

59. See Keene's discussion in *Dawn to the West*, p. 338

60. *Kodansha Encyclopedia of Japan*, 5:350

Tanizaki Jun'ichirō

1. The critics are Mushanokōji Saneatsu (himself, frankly, a rather simple-minded novelist) and Kobayashi Hideo.

2. The list is Anthony H. Chambers', in his article "A Study of Tanizaki's *Shōshō Shigemoto no Haha*," Harvard Journal of Asiatic Studies 1978, p. 357

3. For a useful examination of the wariness of Japanese readers and critics toward Tanizaki, see Okuno Takeo, "*Hyōden-teki kaisetsu*," in the *Tanizaki Jun'ichirō shū* of the Gendai Nihon no Bungaku series (Tokyo: Gakken, 1969), pp. 417–48

4. Chambers, in his study of "*Shigemoto*," borrows the terms from an earlier article by Edward Seidensticker, "Tanizaki Jun-ichirō, 1886–1965," *Monumenta Nipponica* 21 (1966), pp. 249–65

5. Chambers, "*Shigemoto*," p. 357

6. Quoted in Donald Keene, *Dawn to the West*, p. 740

7. A trained anthropologist might be tempted to argue that, in fact, the manner in which male children are reared in Japan, being utterly dependent upon their mothers and thoroughly doted upon, makes this facet of Tanizaki's literature less than abnormal in Japanese society.

8. Edward Fowler, Afterword to his translation of Tanizaki's "*Haha o kouru ki*" (Longing for Mother), *Monumenta Nipponica* XXXV, 4 (1980), p. 481

9. See Donald Keene, *Dawn to the West*, p. 722

10. Tanizaki, *Childhood Years*, trans. by Paul McCarthy (Tokyo: Kodansha International, 1988), p. 20

11. Ibid., p. 100

12. Ibid., p. 107

13. It is probably worth noting that Seiji, in the remarks quoted above, declared, "I think that of all her children, mother loved me the most."

14. Quoted in the chronology in Nakamura Mitsuo, *Tanizaki Jun'ichirō ron*, Kindai Sakka Kenkyū Sōsho 39 (Tokyo: Nihon Tosho Sentaa, 1984), p. 210

15. *Childhood Years*, p. 14

16. Ibid., p. 32

17. The first four years of elementary school (*shōgakkō jinjōka*) were separated from the upper (*kōtō*) four; I will maintain the distinction by using the terms "primary school" and "intermediate school."

18. *Childhood Years*, p. 39

19. Noted in the reminiscences of one of Tanizaki's childhood friends, Hamamoto Hiroshi, as quoted in Nakamura, *Tanizaki Jun'ichirō ron*, p. 211

20. *Childhood Years*, p. 70. This is the recollection of Tanizaki's school friend, Sasanuma Gennosuke.

21. Ibid., p. 43

22. Ibid., p. 80

23. Ibid., pp.63–4

24. Ibid., p. 176

25. Ibid., p. 160

26. Tanizaki's brother, Seiji, has written that in those days only about ten percent of the students who finished intermediate school went on to middle school, and that most of the merchant families sent their sons out as shop clerks as soon as they graduated from intermediate school. See Tanizaki Seiji, "*Ani to watakushi no shōnen jidai*," in the bulletin included in the *Tanizaki Jun'ichirō shū* of the Gendai Nihon no Bungaku series, p. 8.

27. Related in the chronology in Nakamura, *Tanizaki Jun'ichirō ron*, p. 220

28. Keene, *Dawn to the West*, p. 725

29. Quoted in the chronology in Nakamura, *Tanizaki Jun'ichirō ron*, p. 223

30. Ibid., pp. 223–4. Though always interested in the flesh, Tanizaki was never athletic; in 1912, when he reported for his required conscription physical, he was rejected by the military for being "too fat."

31. Hamamoto's observations are quoted in Nakamura, *Tanizaki Jun'ichirō ron*, p. 226

32. *Childhood Years*, p. ix

33. Tanizaki Seiji reports that his brother Jun'ichirō was the only graduating senior at his high school who went on to the university. See "*Ani to watakushi*," p. 8

34. Keene, *Dawn to the West*, p. 726

35. *Childhood Years*, p. 75

36. In actuality, this was a revival of a previously existing literary journal. It is not uncommon for Japanese literary journals in the modern period to pass through a series of brief incarnations over the years.

37. From the reminiscences of Gotō Sueo, a novelist and scholar of French literature, quoted in Nakamura, *Tanizaki Jun'ichirō ron*, p. 228

38. Gotō speculates that the government, which used the excuse that proper licenses for sale had not been obtained, censored the magazine simply because they had lost patience with confessional writings by the Naturalists, who dominated most college campuses at the time, and had decided to trample indiscriminately on all young university writers. For an excellent account of Japanese censorship of literature in the modern period, see Jay Rubin, Injurious to Public Morals: Writers and the Meiji State (Seattle: University of Washington Press, 1984)

39. Keene, *Dawn to the West*, p. 733

40. Ibid., p. 732

41. See discussions of these points in Keene, *Dawn to the West*, p. 732, and Seidensticker, "Tanizaki Jun-ichirō," p. 253

42. The *Tattooer* collection was taken up as a possible recipient of the literary prize offered by the Ministry of Education that year, the judges for which prize included Mori Ōgai and Shimamura Hōgetsu. See Keene, *Dawn to the West*, p. 733, and note 30

43. Nakamura, *Tanizaki Jun'ichirō ron*, p. 221

44. Hamamoto, quoted in Nakamura, *Tanizaki Jun'ichirō ron*, pp. 232–3. Hamamoto also relates an amusing story of a robber who broke into the Kai-

rakuen one night when Tanizaki was staying there. When the household was awakened by shouts that a thief had fled with someone's satchel, Tanizaki turned pale, and he alone breathed a sigh of relief when it was discovered that the satchel belonged to Sasanuma Gennosuke and contained "only money." The following day, Tanizaki, to the great amusement of everyone present, demand stylistic changes in the report that was being prepared for the police.

45. Translation by Anthony H. Chambers, from his introduction to his translation of Tanizaki's *Naomi* (New York: Alfred A. Knopf, 1985), viii

46. Most likely not the Fukuko who had been instrumental in getting Tanizaki kicked out of the Kitamuras' house; Fukuko died in 1912, and this new affair seems to have been around 1913.

47. Quoted from the memoirs of Tatsuno, in Nakamura, *Tanizaki Jun'ichirō ron*, p. 235

48. Keene, *Dawn to the West*, p. 734

49. Ibid., p. 741

50. See, for instance, Keene, *Dawn to the West*, p. 738

51. By now, Kuragorō had taken over the rice shop that was previously operated by his full brother, Kyūbei. In August of 1915 Kyūbei, in despair over his inability to control the behavior of his son, committed suicide by throwing himself from a boat bound for Izu Ōshima.

52. Keene, *Landscapes and Portraits* (Tokyo: Kodansha International, 1971), p. 179

53. Translation by Edward Fowler, from his Afterword to "Longing for Mother," pp. 481–2

54. Joseph L. Anderson and Donald Richie, *The Japanese Film: Art and Industry* (Princeton: Princeton University Press, 1982), p. 40

55. Translation by Anthony Chambers, from his introduction to *Naomi*, pp. vi-vii

56. Keene, *Landscapes and Portraits*, p. 171

57. The Osaka *Asahi Shinbun*, where he would begin to serialize *Naomi* in March 1924.

58. Keene, *Dawn to the West*, p. 750

59. Some of this reaction is noted in Keene, *Landscapes and Portraits*, p. 314

60. Keene, *Dawn to the West*, p. 744

61. Keene, *Landscapes and Portraits*, pp. 179–80

62. Keene, *Dawn to the West*, p. 783, n. 89

63. One of Tanizaki's translators tells of going disco dancing in Tokyo with Matsuko when she was in her seventies.

64. Matsuko herself is unclear about this; she feels that this may have been a second meeting, and that their initial encounter was as early as November 1926.

66. With his earnings from the collection, he built himself a lavish Chinese-style home near Kobe in 1928. See Keene, *Dawn to the West*, p. 757

66. From the writings of novelist Muramatsu Shōfū, quoted in Nakamura, *Tanizaki Jun'ichirō ron*, pp. 263–4

67. Apparently his lovers, in a curious twist on Tanizaki's affair with Chiyo's sister, included Matsuko's sister.

68. Keene, *Dawn to the West*, p. 764

69. Ibid., pp.754–5

70. Translation by Edward Seidensticker, in his article "Tanizaki Jun-ichirō,"

p. 261

71. For a detailed discussion of the debate between Akutagawa and Tanizaki, see the chapter "The Plot Controversy between Tanizaki and Akutagawa," in Noriko Mizuta Lippit, *Reality and Fiction in Modern Japanese Literature* (White Plains: M. E. Sharpe, 1980). Akutagawa committed suicide by purposely downing an overdose of drugs. He was found dead with a well-marked Bible at his bedside.

72. The novel has not been translated into English, and the title is difficult to render, though "maelstrom" seems a good candidate. It is the name for the Buddhist swastika, and as Keene points out in *Landscapes and Portraits*, p. 180, "The curious title is intended to suggest ... the peculiarly twisted relations of the four characters who form the four arms of a swastika."

73. See Chambers, *"Shigemoto,"* p. 374

74. From *Anthology of Sōkyoku and Jiuta Song Texts*, compiled and translated by Gen'ichi Tsuge (Tokyo: Academia Music Ltd., 1983), p. 81

75. Satō's recollections of the series of events is reproduced in Nakamura, *Tanizaki Jun'ichirō ron*, pp. 254–9

76. Satō wrote a famous poem, "Song of the Pike," describing the rather awkward relationships that existed between himself and Tanizaki's family at the outset:

Ah
Autumn wind
If you have any compassion
Go and tell her

That her man
For supper tonight, alone
Ate pike
And thought of her.

Pike, pike ...
Squeeze the sour juice of a green tangerine over it,
Then eat it—that is what they do at his home.
Curious, then fond of this habit,
Time after time she would pick a green tangerine ready for his supper.

Ah
A wife soon to be renounced by her husband and
A man deserted by his wife, facing across the supper table;
A little girl, unloved by her father,
Struggling with her baby chopsticks:
'Give me that juicy bit,' she says, to the man not her father.

Ah
Autumn wind
Take a good look
At this happy gathering not of this world.
Autumn wind, please
Bear witness that this happy gathering

Once was not a dream.
[Translation in Geoffrey Bownas and Anthony Thwaite, trans., *The Penguin Book of Japanese Verse* (Harmondsworth: Penguin Books, 1964), pp. 194–5]

77. Text in Nakamura, *Tanizaki Jun'ichirō ron*, p. 252

78. Ibid.

79. See Chambers' introduction to his translation of *Arrowroot*, which is included in *The Secret History of the Lord of Musashi* (New York: Knopf, 1982), p. vii. Tanizaki made the remark in 1948, after he had written *The Makioka Sisters*.

80. See the article about the discovery of the letters in the March 19, 1986 issue of *Hokubei Mainichi*.

81. See, for instance, Keene, *Dawn to the West*, p. 766

82. Translation by Seidensticker, from his article "Tanizaki Jun-ichirō," p. 255

83. *In Praise of Shadows*, trans. by Thomas J. Harper and Edward G. Seidensticker (New Haven: Leete's Island Books, 1977), pp. 29–30

84. Related both in Seidensticker, "Tanizaki Jun-ichirō," p. 253, and in Thomas J. Harper's afterword to *In Praise of Shadows*, p. 48

85. Quoted in Anthony Chambers, "Postscript to 'A Portrait of Shunkin,'" *Monumenta Nipponica* XXXV, 4 (Winter 1980), p. 458

86. Seidensticker, quoting Nakamura Mitsuo in "Tanizaki Jun-ichirō," p. 258

87. Paul McCarthy, preface to his translation of *A Cat, a Man, and Two Women* (Tokyo: Kodansha International, 1990), p. ix

88. Matsuko's recollection is that this occurred in October of 1938. See Inazawa Hideo, *Tanizaki Jun'ichirō no sekai* (Tokyo: Shichōsha, 1981), p. 299

89. See Keene, *Dawn to the West*, p. 774

90. In his first story, in 1903, Tanizaki had written, "Ever since I was a small child I had disliked military men most of all human beings.... " See Keene, *Dawn to the West*, p. 724

91. Keene, *Landscapes and Portraits*, p. 313. Keene goes on to describe how the journal's editor was summoned before a board of army officers and asked to explain his decision to publish Tanizaki's frivolous work.

92. Keene, *Landscapes and Portraits*, p. 315

93. From Kafū's diary, quoted in Inazawa's chronology, p. 269

94. On a visit to Japan, Jean-Paul Sartre described *The Makioka Sisters* as the novel which most realistically portrayed the essence of modern Japan; he also declared that *The Diary of a Mad Old Man* was the first novel in the world to come to grips with the issue of elderly sexuality. See Okuno Takeo, "*Hyōden-teki kuisetsu*," p. 424

95. Chambers, "*Shigemoto*," p. 361

96. Chambers, in "*Shigemoto*," notes that Tanizaki, who frequently complained of being a slow writer and could normally produce only two or three pages of writing a day, completed *Shigemoto* between April and December of 1949, before the first installment even appeared in the newspaper.

97. The most recent film adaptation of *Sasameyuki*, by the renowned director Ichikawa Kon, attempts to insinuate some of Tanizaki's private playfulness by having Sachiko's husband, Teinosuke, make advances to Yukiko, and in the final scene, as a "thin snow" falls outside his window, Teinosuke collapses into tears as Yukiko heads off to be married. This interpolation completely spoils

Tanizaki's story.

98. See Okuno Takeo, "*Hyōden-teki kaisetsu*," p. 424

99. Keene, *Dawn to the West*, p. 721

100. Ibid., pp.744–5

101. Keene, *Landscapes and Portraits*, p. 174. The essay, "*Kawaya no iroiro*" (All about Toilets), was published by Tanizaki in 1935. It is probably also worth recalling in this connection that the final line of *The Makioka Sisters* reminds us of Yukiko's humanity by describing her struggles with diarrhea as she sets out to be married.

Kawabata Yasunari

1. "*Bungaku-teki jijōden*," in the Kawabata volume of the Chikuma Gendai Bungaku Taikei, vol. 32 (Tokyo: Chikuma Shobō, 1975), p. 455

2. See, for instance, Hasegawa Izumi, *Kawabata Yasunari ronkō*, 3rd expanded and revised edition (Tokyo: Meiji Shoin, 1984), p. 481

3. See the story "*Abura*" in the *Kawabata Yasunari zenshū*, 35 vols. (Tokyo: Shinchōsha, 1980–83), 2:66

4. "*Fubo e no tegami*," *Zenshū* 5:225

5. "*Abura*," *Zenshū* 2:64; also described in "*Sōshiki no meijin*," 2:76

6. From the story "*Sobo*," *Zenshū* 2:439–40

7. On this topic, see the article by Tezuka Tomio, "*Hito to bungaku*," in the Chikuma Kawabata volume, p. 482

8. "*Fubo e no tegami*," *Zenshū* 5:221. See also the description in "*Sobo*."

9. These thoughts are recorded in "*Fubo e no tegami*," *Zenshū* 5:223

10. Ibid., p. 224

11. Ibid., p. 203

12. Translation by J. Martin Holman, from *Palm-of-the-Hand Stories*, trans. by Lane Dunlop and J. Martin Holman (San Francisco: North Point Press, 1988), pp. 3–4

13. From Mishima's famous article on Kawabata, "*Eien no tabibito*," quoted in Furuya Tsunatake, *Hyōden Kawabata Yasunari* (Tokyo: Jitsugyō no Nihon Sha, 1960), p. 53

14. "*Fubo e no tegami*," *Zenshū* 5:212

15. From Kawabata, "*Shōsetsu no kenkyū*," quoted in Furuya, pp. 61–2

16. See Kawabata, "*Jūrokusai no nikki*," *Zenshū* 2:24

17. "*Fubo e no tegami*," *Zenshū* 5:208–9

18. From *Shōnen*; quoted in Furuya, p. 67

19. Ibid., p. 68

20. The publication history of this "Diary of My Sixteenth Year" is complex, and there is some degree of doubt that it was actually written when Kawabata claims it was. Some scholars are of the opinion that it was composed when Kawabata actually published it, in 1925. For the study of Kawabata's life, however, the document must be considered as reliable as anything else he wrote about his own private experience.

21. Grandfather had, in fact, written a manuscript on "house divination," but

was frustrated in his attempts to get it published.

22. From an unpublished translation of "*Jūrokusai no nikki*" by J. Martin Holman

23. "*Fubo e no tegami*," *Zenshū* 5:228–9

24. "*Sōshiki*," *Zenshū* 2:78

25. Quoted, with revisions, from Holman, trans., "Diary of My Sixteenth Year"

26. "*Sōshiki*," *Zenshū* 2:78

27. Ibid., p. 79

28. "*Fubo e no tegami*," *Zenshū* 5:216–17

29. From the 1948–52 work, *Shōnen*, quoted in Furuya, p. 97

30. Ibid., p. 102

31. Ibid., p. 104

32. See *Shōnen*, *Zenshū* 10:228

33. Phrases Kawabata used repeatedly in his fiction, these are found in close proximity in "*Izu no odoriko*"

34. These thoughts are expressed in the stories "*Abura*" and "*Sōshiki no meijin*," as well as in "*Fubo e no tegami*"

35. One of Kawabata's close friends and literary associates from this period, Ishihama Kinsaku, noted in his memoirs that Kawabata was absolutely fearless about calling on famous writers and editors. His imperturbability aroused the envy of Ishihama, who was surprised that an Osaka person could outdo a Tokyoite in chutzpah. See Furuya, pp. 140–42

36. Ibid., p. 141

37. Ibid., pp.141–2

38. A full critical study, *Yokomitsu Riichi: Modernist*, has been written by Dennis Keene. Kawabata describes in his "*Bungaku-teki jijōden*" how deeply indebted he was to Yokomitsu's friendship; he claims that when Yokomitsu was invited to join the editorial staff at the magazine *Bungaku*, he agreed to do so only if they would also invite Kawabata. "*Bungaku-teki jijōden*," p. 461

39. It should be noted that the university calendar underwent major changes in Japan this year; the beginning of the new academic year was moved to April, meaning that Kawabata's first "year" of classes only encompassed seven months

40. Kawabata records this remarkable incident in "*Bungaku-teki jijōden*," p. 453

41. "*Fubo e no tegami*," *Zenshū* 5:189. Kawabata goes on to describe his own obligatory conscription physical: worried that he would be criticized for his weak constitution, Kawabata spent a month before the exam at an Izu hot spring resort, resting and exercising and downing nearly a dozen raw eggs a day. Even so, the army doctor berated him, snarling, "What good's a literary type with a body like yours going to be for the nation?"

42. Quoted in Tezuka, p. 485

43. Quoted in Donald Keene, *Dawn to the West* (New York: Holt, Rinehart and Winston, 1984), pp. 794–5

44. From "*Nampō no hi*," quoted in Furuya, p. 109

45. Quoted in Tezuka, p. 486

46. Nakagawa Yoichi, quoted in Furuya, p. 139

47. Ibid., p. 155

48. Ibid., p. 162

49. The Galsworthy story Kawabata chose to translate was "The Road." His Chekhov selection, "After the Theatre" (Posle teatra) of 1892, is most interesting. Kawabata had already written a story about his doomed love affair with "Chiyo," and one can only imagine the feelings that coursed through him as he translated the Chekhov story, which is about a fickle sixteen-year-old girl who toys with the hearts of two men. She returns home after seeing Yevgeny Onyegin, and Chekhov describes the scene as follows:

> She was only sixteen and did not yet love anyone. She knew that an officer called Gorny and a student called Gruzdev loved her, but now after the opera she wanted to be doubtful of their love. To be unloved and unhappy—how interesting that was. There is something beautiful, touching, and poetical about it when one loves and the other is indifferent. Onyegin was interesting because he was not in love at all, and Tatyana was fascinating because she was so much in love; but if they had been equally in love with each other and had been happy, they would perhaps have seemed dull.
>
> "Leave off declaring that you love me," Nadya went on writing, thinking of Gorny. "I cannot believe it. You are very clever, cultivated, serious, you have immense talent, and perhaps a brilliant future awaits you, while I am an uninteresting girl of no importance, and you know very well that I should be only a hindrance in your life. It is true that you were attracted by me and thought you had found your ideal in me, but that was a mistake, and now you are asking yourself in despair: 'Why did I meet that girl?' And only your goodness of heart prevents you from owning it to yourself...."

[Translation by Constance Garnett. From *The Schoolmistress and Other Stories*, by Anton Chekhov (New York: The Ecco Press, 1986), pp. 81–2]

50. An amusing and revealing anecdote about the cold, penetrating expression in Kawabata's eyes comes from 1928, when he was living in Atami. The writer Kajii Motojirō had stopped off to spend the night at Kawabata's residence. That night a robber broke into the house, but through the darkness the intruder's gaze met that of the awakened Kawabata. Muttering only, "So it's no good, eh?" the robber fled. The incident is related in the chronology in the *Zenshū*, 35:474

51. Quoted in Keene, *Dawn to the West*, p. 796

52. Kawabata's story "*Sōshiki no meijin*" (The Master of Funerals) was published in May of that same year.

53. See "*Bungaku-teki jijōden*," p. 459

54. Quoted in Keene, *Dawn to the West*, p. 793

55. From Seidensticker's entry on Kawabata in the *Kodansha Encyclopedia of Japan*, 4:175

56. Quoted in the commentary appended to a paperback collection of his palm-of-the-hand stories, *Tenohira no shōsetsu* (Tokyo: Shinchōsha, Shinchō Bunko, 1971), p. 495. It is perhaps worth noting that many critics transliterate this title as "*Tanagokoro no shōsetsu*." Both pronunciations are correct; I have merely followed the transliteration given in this particular volume.

57. A curious footnote: careful readers of Kawabata's fiction translated into English may notice that the copyrights to his works are sometimes listed as

owned by "Hite Kawabata," a most un-Japanese sounding name. In fact, Hideko is listed in her family registry simply as "Hite" (a misprint, perhaps?), and that name is sometimes used in copyright declarations. Kawabata's estate has no connection with the Hite Report.

58. Joseph L. Anderson and Donald Richie, *The Japanese Film: Art and Industry*, expanded edition (Princeton: Princeton University Press, 1982), pp. 54–5

59. Like his palm-of-the-hand stories, the films based on Kawabata's works, for which he did not write the screenplays himself, are clustered in several time periods. Some six films were made in the 1930s; a revival of interest in his work led to over a dozen film treatments in the 1950s, and production continued at the rate of at least one per year after that.

60. The 1954 version of "The Izu Dancer" starred Misora Hibari, one of the most popular singers of the postwar era; the actress Yoshinaga Sayuri played the dancing girl in the 1963 edition, and more recently popular singer Yamaguchi Momoe attempted the role.

61. Kawabata most certainly romanticized much of his own experience from the journey. He admitted, in an essay published when one of the film adaptations was made, that he had purposely omitted some of the uglier details about members of the performing troupe, thereby making it more persuasive when they concluded he was a "good person." He did not mention, for instance, that the husband and wife in the troupe were suffering from abscesses that were the result of a foul disease, and that the sight of them changing the medicine plasters on their diseased limbs in the hot water of the springs made him hesitant to enter the bath himself. See the discussion of this in Furuya, pp. 173–4

62. "*Fubo e no tegami*," *Zenshū* 5:184–7

63. Among the well-known writers living in Magome at the time were Hirotsu Kazuo, Muroo Saisei, Makino Shin'ichi, Uno Chiyo, and Hagiwara Sakutarō. Kawabata commented that he went out for walks so often with Uno Chiyo that some people mistook them for lovers. Many years later, Mishima Yukio would build his Spanish villa-style house in Magome.

64. He took an intense personal interest in fostering the dance ambitions of one woman, Umezono Tatsuko, at the Casino; he arranged for her to take Western dancing lessons from an American dancer, and sent her to an English-language school. He got her into a dance troupe, tried to get her trained as a ballerina, and helped her get a role in the film version of his *Asakusa no shimai* (Sisters from Asakusa) in 1935.

65. Keene, *Dawn to the West*, p. 810. The specific time period Keene has reference to is around 1933, when Kawabata composed "*Kinjū*" (Of Birds and Beasts)

66. "*Fubo e no tegami*," *Zenshū* 5:194–99. The attraction to the sister of the woman he loved would reappear in somewhat reconstructed form in *The Sound of the Mountain*.

67. Kawabata served as editor for the posthumous two-volume collection of Hōjō's writings.

68. "*Bungaku-teki jijōden*," p. 459

69. Keene, *Dawn to the West*, pp. 802–3

70. As Keene notes, Dazai wanted the prize not only for the fame it would bring him, but also because the cash award would help him buy the drugs he craved. *Dawn to the West*, p. 1042

71. Translation by Phyllis I. Lyons, from her book *The Saga of Dazai Osamu* (Stanford: Stanford University Press, 1985), pp. 37–8

72. Translation by Keene, *Dawn to the West*, p. 1043. Keene also points out that Dazai assumed when he wrote his attack on Kawabata that it was "Flowers of Buffoonery" and not "Against the Current" that had been rejected by the jury.

73. Keene, *Dawn to the West*, p. 1044

74. Quoted in Furuya, pp. 221–2

75. After the first two "linked stories" in January of 1935, Kawabata published two more at the end of the same year; another two in 1936; one in 1937, after which a "story collection" titled *Snow Country* appeared in book form. Two more stories were written in 1940–41. New sections were added in 1946 and 1947, and the version which was translated into English was published in December of 1948.

76. From, interestingly enough, the Literary Discussion Group of which he was a member.

77. The friend, in fact, was the *go* master, Shūsai. In January of 1940, Kawabata visited the master and played a couple of games with him. Two days later Shūsai was dead, and Kawabata captured his dead visage on film. In 1938 Kawabata would embark on two "photography journeys," one of them to take pictures of the setting for Tayama Katai's novel *Country Teacher*.

78. Of this "chronicle-novel," Edward Seidensticker has written: "The defeat of the master is made to seem the defeat of a great tradition, and it can be seen as an oblique comment on Japan's disastrous defeat in 1945, by which Kawabata was deeply affected." *Kodansha Encyclopedia of Japan*, 4:176

79. Keene, *Dawn to the West*, pp. 819–20

80. Ibid., p. 819

81. Donald Keene, *Landscapes and Portraits* (Tokyo: Kodansha International, 1971), p. 314

82. Keene, *Dawn to the West*, p. 824. His other reading during the war years included *The Pillow Book of Sei Shōnagon*, the *Hōjōki* of Kamo no Chōmei, Kenkō's *Essays in Idleness*, Saikaku, Chikamatsu, and the haiku poets. See Masao Miyoshi, *Accomplices of Silence: The Modern Japanese Novel* (Berkeley: University of California Press, 1974), pp. 112–13

83. Besides Kawabata himself, major contributors included Kume Masao, Kobayashi Hideo, and Takami Jun.

84. Keene, *Dawn to the West*, p. 823

85. The quote is from Nakamura Mitsuo; cited in Tezuka, p. 490

86. Kawabata's very personal eulogy at Yokomitsu's funeral is particularly poignant. After suggesting that the war and defeat crushed Yokomitsu's body and soul, he concludes: "Yokomitsu—I will go on living, the mountains and rivers of Japan as my soul." Keene, *Dawn to the West*, p. 825

87. Ibid., pp.827–8

88. "Kawabata once called *Snow Country* a 'work that could have been completed at any point.' He said elsewhere, however, that he had wanted to include the fire scene 'even while [he was] writing the earlier sections.' As if to make the provisional nature of his structure still plainer, he also said that *Snow Country* might better have ended without the last sections—that is, those corresponding to the last twenty-five pages in Edward Seidensticker's translation." Miyoshi, p. 104, n.

89. Tōson was followed by Masamune Hakuchō, then Shiga Naoya. Since Kawabata's time, PEN presidents have included Onozawa Kōjirō, Nakamura Mitsuo, Ishikawa Tatsuzō, Takahashi Kenji, Inoue Yasushi, Endō Shūsaku,

and Ōoka Makoto.

90. Yamamoto Kenkichi, "*Kaisetsu,*" *Yama no oto* (Tokyo: Shinchōsha, Shinchō Bunko, 1957), p. 318

91. These are untranslated novels such as *Niji ikutabi* (How Many Times, the Rainbow, 1950–51), *Hi mo tsuki mo* (Days and Months, 1952–53), *Tokyo no hito* (Tokyo People, 1954–55), and *Onna de aru koto* (To Be a Woman, 1956–57). Needless to say, perhaps, all of these works were made into popular films.

92. There can be no question that the Japanese title of Kawabata's speech, "*Utsukushii Nihon no watakushi,*" is virtually untranslatable, but the use of commas in the published English version to divide the main elements into three separate parts (Japan; that which is beautiful; and Kawabata) is the exact opposite of the unifying effect carried by the original Japanese, which literally means something like "I who am a part of beautiful Japan."

93. Translation by Edward Seidensticker, from *Japan, the Beautiful, and Myself* (Tokyo: Kodansha International, 1969), pp. 68–9

94. Kawabata, "*Mishima Yukio,*" *Zenshū* 29:617

95. The letter is to be found in Supplement 2 of the *Zenshū*, pp. 371–2

96. A host of theories have been thrown out for curiosity-seekers. In 1977 the critic Usui Yoshimi published a novel about Kawabata's death suggesting that Kawabata had become obsessed with the young woman who was serving as a maid in his household, and that his despair over the futility of that relationship had been the direct cause of his suicide. The Kawabata family sued Usui for invasion of privacy, but the matter was settled out of court. Kawabata's letter to Harold Strauss, cited above in note 95 and written on April 3, 1972, might be of interest to those who wish to read his death as a suicide. Knopf had been holding Kawabata's royalties from translations of his fiction in an account for him. His letter asks that the total sum of his royalties be sent to him as quickly as possible. He writes, "I don't know how much in US dollars the royalties will amount to, but I imagine it will be sufficient to be of great help to me." It is difficult to think how Kawabata could have been in financial straits, or that a Japanese publisher would not have stepped in immediately with manuscript advances had he been.The request could easily be interpreted as the act of someone wishing to settle all financial loose ends before embarking on an act of self-destruction. But perhaps this speculation is no more enlightening than any other.

97. Inoue in many respects saw himself as a chosen successor to Kawabata: he served as Japan PEN president, was elected an international vice president of that organization, and before his death in 1991, was frequently mentioned on the short list for the Nobel Prize.

98. "*Fubo e no tegami,*" *Zenshū* 5:191

2882

Literature

ACTS OF WORSHIP Seven Stories
Yukio Mishima / Translated by John Bester

These seven consistently interesting stories, each with its own distinctive atmosphere and mood, are a timely reminder of Mishima the consummate writer.

THE SHŌWA ANTHOLOGY
Modern Japanese Short Stories
Edited by Van C. Gessel / Tomone Matsumoto

These 25 superbly translated short stories offer rare and valuable insights into Japanese literature and society. All written in the Shōwa era (1926-1989).

THE HOUSE OF NIRE
Morio Kita / Translated by Dennis Keene

A comic novel that captures the essence of Japanese society while chronicling the lives of the Nire family and their involvement in the family-run mental hospital.

REQUIEM A Novel
Shizuko Gō / Translated by Geraldine Harcourt

A best seller in Japanese, this moving requiem for war victims won the Akutagawa Prize and voiced the feelings of a generation of Japanese women.

A CAT, A MAN, AND TWO WOMEN
Jun'ichiro Tanizaki / Translaned by Paul McCarthy

Lightheartedness and comic realism distinguish this wonderful collection—a novella (the title story) and two shorter pieces. The eminent Tanizaki at his best.

CHILD OF FORTUNE A Novel
Yūko Tsushima / Translated by Geraldine Harcourt

Awarded the Women's Literature Prize, *Child of Fortune* offers a penetrating look at a divorced mother's reluctant struggle against powerful, conformist social pressures.